Our Creative World

Stories, Poems, Documents,
Art, and Architecture from World History

Our Creative World
Edited by John Notgrass

ISBN 978-1-60999-086-2

Cover Photo Credit: The world at night / NASA Earth Observatory

Cover design by Mary Evelyn McCurdy
Interior design by John Notgrass

Printed in the United States of America

Notgrass Company
975 Roaring River Road
Gainesboro, TN 38562
1-800-211-8793
www.notgrass.com

Our Creative World

Many people think history is a lot of names, dates, battles, faraway places and flat pictures of stiff people who never smile. That is not history. History is vibrant color, strong feelings, hopes, dreams, losses, and mysteries. Even the people who are famous in history are still people: normal, interesting, regular, important people, like us. Did you ever stop to think that YOU are a person in history, too? What would you want the student of the future to know about you and your time?

History records Julius Caesar's rise to power, but also the memory that he was bald and embarrassed about it (see page 26). The Ming Dynasty of China is part of history, but so is the woman of that day who left us a wistful poem about parting with loved ones (see page 69). London's Great Fire is an important historical event, but a real person who was there took time to notice and write down the impact the fire had on the city's pigeons (see page 93). Yes, history calls Florence Nightingale the mother of modern nursing, but she also wrote letters to friends when all she could find to write with was a pencil (see page 115).

These pages let the people of history speak for themselves. These are the letters, stories, art, games, sports, recipes, poems, speeches, structures, and memories that were part of their normal, interesting, regular, important lives. Listen to what these voices from history have to say to you and find those stiff, flat people from history come suddenly to life.

Table of Contents

Of the Father's Love Begotten

Aurelius Prudentius (c. 400 AD)

Aurelius Prudentius (c. 348-413) was born in Hispania Tarraconensis, a Roman province that is now in northern Spain. He worked as a lawyer and public official before retiring to a simple life of prayer and fasting. He composed many poems, including the one featured below. This English translation from the original Latin is from the 1850s. John M. Neale made the original translation, which Henry W. Baker revised.

Of the Father's love begotten, ere the worlds began to be,
He is Alpha and Omega, He the source, the ending He,
Of the things that are, that have been,
And that future years shall see, evermore and evermore!

At His Word the worlds were framèd; He commanded; it was done:
Heaven and earth and depths of ocean in their threefold order one;
All that grows beneath the shining
Of the moon and burning sun, evermore and evermore!

He is found in human fashion, death and sorrow here to know,
That the race of Adam's children doomed by law to endless woe,
May not henceforth die and perish
In the dreadful gulf below, evermore and evermore!

O that birth forever blessèd, when the virgin, full of grace,
By the Holy Ghost conceiving, bare the Savior of our race;
And the Babe, the world's Redeemer,
First revealed His sacred face, evermore and evermore!

This is He Whom seers in old time chanted of with one accord;
Whom the voices of the prophets promised in their faithful word;
Now He shines, the long expected,
Let creation praise its Lord, evermore and evermore!

O ye heights of heaven adore Him; angel hosts, His praises sing;
Powers, dominions, bow before Him, and extol our God and King!
Let no tongue on earth be silent,
Every voice in concert sing, evermore and evermore!

Righteous judge of souls departed, righteous King of them that live,
On the Father's throne exalted none in might with Thee may strive;
Who at last in vengeance coming
Sinners from Thy face shalt drive, evermore and evermore!

Thee let old men, thee let young men, thee let boys in chorus sing;
Matrons, virgins, little maidens, with glad voices answering:
Let their guileless songs re-echo,
And the heart its music bring, evermore and evermore!

Christ, to Thee with God the Father, and, O Holy Ghost, to Thee,
Hymn and chant with high thanksgiving, and unwearied praises be:
Honor, glory, and dominion,
And eternal victory, evermore and evermore!

This image of Christ from around the time of Prudentius is from the catacomb of Commodilla in Rome. It features Alpha and Omega, the first and last letters of the Greek alphabet.

Ancient Hawaiian Poetry

The early settlers of the Hawaiian islands came from the Polynesian culture of the Pacific Ocean. Recognizing the beauty of the natural world was an important part of this culture. These two excerpts were collected and translated by Nathaniel B. Emerson. He was born in Oahu, Hawaii, in 1839; his father was a missionary. Dr. Emerson's book Unwritten Literature of Hawaii *was published in 1909.*

Black crabs are climbing,
Crabs from the great sea,
Sea that is darkling.
Black crabs and gray crabs
Scuttle o'er the reef-plate.
Billows are tumbling and lashing,
Beating and surging nigh.
Sea-shells are crawling up;
And lurking in holes
Are the eels o-u and o-i.
But taste the sea-weed a-kaha-kaha.
Ka-hiki! how the sea rages!
The wild sea of Kane!

'Twas in Ko'o-lau I met with the rain:
It comes with lifting and tossing of dust,
Advancing in columns, dashing along.
The rain, it sighs in the forest;
The rain, it beats and whelms, like the surf;
It smites, it smites now the land.
Pasty the earth from the stamping rain;
Full run the streams, a rushing flood;
The mountain wall leaps with the rain.
See the water chafing its bounds like a dog,
A raging dog, gnawing its way to pass out.

Hawaiian Black Crab

An Account of Egypt
Herodotus (c. 440 BC)

Herodotus was a Greek historian who compiled an extensive record of cultures and nations that bordered the eastern part of the Mediterranean Sea. The following excerpt contains his description of the building of the Great Pyramid of Giza under Pharaoh Khufu (also known as Cheops). This 1904 translation is by George Campbell Macaulay.

For the making of the pyramid itself there passed a period of twenty years; and the pyramid is square, each side measuring eight hundred feet, and the height of it is the same. It is built of stone smoothed and fitted together in the most perfect manner, not one of the stones being less than thirty feet in length.

This pyramid was made after the manner of steps which some called "rows" and others "bases": and when they had first made it thus, they raised the remaining stones with machines made of short pieces of timber, raising them first from the ground to the first stage of the steps, and when the stone got up to this it was placed upon another machine standing on the first stage, and so from this it was drawn to the second upon another machine; for as many as were the courses of the steps, so many machines there were also, or perhaps they transferred one and the same machine, made so as easily to be carried, to each stage successively, in order that they might take up the stones; for let it be told in both ways, according as it is reported.

However that may be the highest parts of it were finished first, and afterwards they proceeded to finish that which came next to them, and lastly they finished the parts of it near the ground and the lowest ranges.

On the pyramid it is declared in Egyptian writing how much was spent on radishes and onions and leeks for the workmen, and if I rightly remember that which the interpreter said in reading to me this inscription, a sum of one thousand six hundred talents of silver was spent; and if this is so, how much besides is likely to have been expended upon the iron with which they worked, and upon bread and clothing for the workmen, seeing that they were building the works for the time which has been mentioned and were occupied for no small time besides, as I suppose, in the cutting and bringing of the stones and in working at the excavation under the ground?

Eduard Spelterini took this photo from a balloon in 1904. The Great Pyramid is on the right.

Chronicle of the Reign of Sargon

This description of Sargon's reign comes from a tablet written about 600 BC, though it is thought to be a copy of a much earlier record. This excerpt is from A Source-Book of Ancient History (1912), *published by husband and wife team George and Lillie Botsford.*

The text refers to Ishtar and Marduk, the names of two false gods worshipped in the Middle East. Kasalla and Subartu are the names of places that Sargon attacked, while Agade is the name of a town Sargon controlled.

Sargon, King of Akkad, through the royal gift of Ishtar was exalted, and he possessed no foe nor rival. His glory over the world he poured out. The Sea in the East[*] he crossed, and in the eleventh year the Country of the West in its full extent his hand subdued. He united them under one control; he set up his images in the West; their booty he brought over at his word. The sons of his palace for five *kasbu*[**] around he settled, and over the hosts of the world he reigned supreme.

Against Kasalla he marched, and he turned Kasalla into mounds and heaps of ruins; he destroyed the land and left not enough for a bird to rest thereon. Afterward in his old age all the lands revolted against him, and they besieged him in Agade; and Sargon went forth to battle and defeated them; he accomplished their overthrow, and their widespreading host he destroyed.

Afterward he attacked the land of Subartu in his might, and they submitted to his arms, and Sargon settled that revolt, and defeated them; he accomplished their overthrow, and their widespreading host he destroyed, and he brought their possessions into Agade. The soil from the trenches of Babylon he removed, and the boundaries of Agade he made like those of Babylon. But because of the evil which he had committed the great lord Marduk was angry, and he destroyed his people by famine. From the rising of the sun unto the setting of the sun they opposed him and gave him no rest.

---

[*] *The Persian Gulf*
[**] *About seven miles*

Board Games of Sumer and Egypt

These photos illustrate two of the oldest known board games. The game in the top photo is called the Royal Game of Ur or the Game of Twenty Squares. Two copies were found in the Royal Tombs of Ur in Iraq. The game in the bottom photo is an Egyptian game called Senet. This example is from the tomb of Pharaoh Tutankhamun, though older examples have also been found.

Archaeologists do not know exactly how the ancient Sumerians and Egyptians played these games, though you can find rules that people have attempted to recreate. The modern game of backgammon appears to have some similarities, in that players use dice to race their pieces around the board.

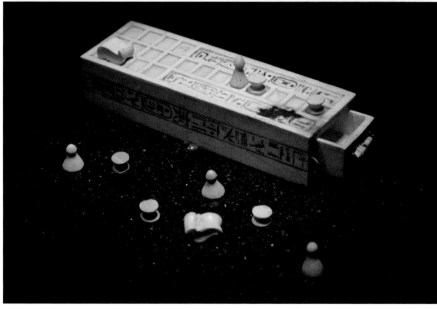

Babylonian Herding Contract
(c. 1700 BC)

This contract was recorded on a Babylonian tablet during the reign of King Samsuiluna, a son of Hammurabi. It is similar to the agreement between Laban and Jacob, through which Laban entrusted care of his flocks to Jacob and Jacob was responsible for any losses. This translation by J. J. Finkelstein (1922-1974) was published in "An Old Babylonian Herding Contract and Genesis 31:38 f," Journal of the American Oriental Society, Vol. 88, No. 1 (Jan. - Mar., 1968), pp. 30-36.

92 ewes, 20 rams, 22 breeding lambs, 24 spring lambs, 33 she-goats, 4 male goats, 27 kids—total: 158 sheep; total: 64 goats, which Sinsamuh has entrusted to Dada the shepherd. Dada assumes liability (therefore) and will replace any lost (animals). Should Nidnatum, Dada's shepherd boy, absent himself, Nidnatum will bear responsibility for any loss, and Dada will measure out 5 kor of barley.

Three witnesses; Samsuiluna year 1, fourth month, 16th day.

Sheep Herded by a Bedouin Family in Modern Syria

Seal of Tarkummuwa

Hittite (c. 1400 BC)

This Hittite seal was discovered about 1850 at Smyrna, an ancient city in what is now the country of Turkey. It features a man wearing royal robes holding a sword. The text in the center is written in Hittite hieroglyphs. The text around the rim is written in cuneiform. Having the inscription in two languages helped scholars learn how to read the Hittite writing. The seal states that it was created for Tarkummuwa, King of Mera.

Bull-Leaping Fresco
Minoan (c. 1400 BC)

This restored fresco painting is from the Palace of Knossos on the island of Crete. One person is shown leaping over a bull with two other people participating in the action. Archaeologists have debated the origin and purpose of this dangerous practice. Some scholars have suggested that the image is symbolic rather than a depiction of actual events. However, it has some similarities with a sport that still exists in southern France and northern Spain. Known as course landaise, *the goal is for athletes to jump over a charging cow or bull. Unlike modern bullfighting, the animal is not harmed.*

Four Remarkable Things in England
Henry of Huntingdon (c. 1130 AD)

Henry of Huntingdon (c. 1088-1157) was born in England after the Norman conquest of 1066. His father was a Norman church officer. Henry compiled a history of England that included this description of Stonehenge, the earliest known written description of it.

There are four things in England which are very remarkable. One is that the winds issue with such great violence from certain caverns in a mountain called the Peak, that it ejects matters thrown into them, and whirling them about in the air carries them to a great distance. The second is at Stonehenge, where stones of extraordinary dimensions are raised as columns, and others are fixed above, like lintels of immense portals; and no one has been able to discover by what mechanism such vast masses of stone were elevated, nor for what purpose they were designed. The third is at Chedder-hole, where there is a cavern which many persons have entered, and have traversed a great distance under ground, crossing subterraneous streams, without finding any end of the cavern. The fourth wonder is this, that in some parts of the country the rain is seen to gather about the tops of the hills, and forthwith to fall on the plains.

This illustration of Stonehenge is from a 1645 Dutch atlas of the world.

Hymn to the King Wu Ting

Chinese (c. 700s BC)

Wu Ting was a member of the Shang dynasty who ruled from about 1250-1192 BC. This poem comes from a collection honoring Shang rulers. It was apparently written by the 700s BC, though it may be older. This translation is from The Book of Chinese Poetry *(1891) by Clement Francis Romilly Allen. Allen was a British diplomat in China.*

'Twas by a decree of heaven that a swallow was sent to this earth
That the race of Shang might spring from a wondrous and mystic birth,
To dwell in the land of Yin, and mightily rule the land,
Till the people from north to south were submissive to their command.

Then heaven called forth King T'ang, a monarch war-like and bold,
To govern and settle the folk, and to guide them in days of old.
To aid him in this he chose as princes the men of skill,
And regions nine were his vassals, obeying his sovereign will.

Since the first Shang reigned, we trusted that nothing should snatch away
The God-given power bestowed on Wu Ting's offspring to-day.
This scion of Wu Ting's line can fearlessly hold his own.
No foe may dare to assail his crown, or disturb his throne.

With their dragon-blazoned banners above them then princes bring
The mighty bowls of millet to grace this our offering.
The Royal domain itself holds a thousand of miles, and none
Of the folk therein is distressed, and thence do our frontiers run

To the oceans four which surround us, and men from the shore of the seas
Will come to our Court in crowds to share in such rites as these,
And to gaze on the mountain which forms a defence and a fortress meet
For our city girt by the river, which flows at the mountain's feet.

When a King maintains his State and earns all his subjects' love,
We say how wise is the choice of the far-seeing powers above.

Lucky and Unlucky Days
Egyptian (c. 1200 BC)

We believe that God guides what happens each day, not luck. However, the ancient Egyptians believed that certain days were lucky or unlucky. A papyrus written in Egypt around the time of Ramses II has a list of these days. Below are some of the statements from the list. This translation is from The Literature of the Ancient Egyptians *by E.A. Wallis Budge (1914).*

1st day of Hathor. The whole day is lucky. There is festival in heaven with Rā and Hathor.

2nd day of Hathor. The whole day is lucky. The gods go out. The goddess Uatchet comes from Tep to the gods who are in the shrine of the bull, in order to protect the divine members.

3rd day of Hathor. The whole day is lucky.

4th day of Hathor. The whole day is unlucky. The house of the man who goes on a voyage on that day comes to ruin.

6th day of Hathor. The whole day is unlucky. Do not light a fire in thy house on this day, and do not look at one.

18th day of Pharmuthi. The whole day is unlucky. Do not bathe on this day.

20th day of Pharmuthi. The whole day is unlucky. Do not work on this day.

22nd day of Pharmuthi. The whole day is unlucky. He who is born on this day will die on this day.

23rd day of Pharmuthi. The first two-thirds of the day are unlucky, and the last third lucky.

One of the Egyptian gods, Apis, had the form of a bull. Some specially-selected bulls that served in religious rituals were mummified on their death.

The Iliad
Homer (c. 800 BC)

This brief excerpt is from the translation of The Iliad *by English poet Alexander Pope (1720).*

Meantime the Grecians in a ring beheld
The coursers bounding o'er the dusty field.
The first who mark'd them was the Cretan king;
High on a rising ground, above the ring,
The monarch sat: from whence with sure survey
He well observed the chief who led the way,
And heard from far his animating cries,
And saw the foremost steed with sharpen'd eyes;
On whose broad front a blaze of shining white,
Like the full moon, stood obvious to the sight.
He saw; and rising, to the Greeks begun:
"Are yonder horse discern'd by me alone?
Or can ye, all, another chief survey,
And other steeds than lately led the way?"

*This statue of Homer is located at the
Bavarian State Library in Munich, Germany.*

Gold Mining
Diodorus Siculus (c. 30 BC)

The Book of Job talks about mining for metals underground (Job 28:1-11), which indicates that it has a long history. Diodorus Siculus was a Greek historian who compiled a forty-volume collection called Library of History *between 60 and 30 BC. He described the terrible conditions of miners. King Solomon imported gold from Ophir (1 Kings 9:28), an unknown location that might have been in Africa. This translation by C. H. Oldfather is taken from the* Loeb Classical Library.

At the extremity of Egypt and in the contiguous territory of both Arabia and Ethiopia there lies a region which contains many large gold mines, where the gold is secured in great quantities with much suffering and at great expense. For the earth is naturally black and contains seams and veins of a marble which is unusually white and in brilliancy surpasses everything else which shines brightly by its nature, and here the overseers of the labour in the mines work to recover the gold with the aid of a multitude of workers.

For the kings of Egypt gather together and condemn to the mining of the gold such as have been found guilty of some crime and captives of war, as well as those who have been accused unjustly and thrown into prison because of their anger, and not only such persons but occasionally all their relatives as well, by this means not only inflicting punishment upon those found guilty but also securing at the same time great revenues from their labours.

And those who have been condemned in this way—and they are a great multitude and are all bound in chains—work at their task unceasingly both by day and throughout the entire night, enjoying no respite and being carefully cut off from any means of escape; since guards of foreign soldiers who speak a language different from theirs stand watch over them, so that not a man, either by conversation or by some contact of a friendly nature, is able to corrupt one of his keepers.

The gold-bearing earth which is hardest they first burn with a hot fire, and when they have crumbled it in this way they continue the working of it by hand; and the soft rock which can yield to moderate effort is crushed with a sledge by myriads of unfortunate wretches. And the entire operations are in charge of a skilled worker who distinguishes the stone and points it out to the labourers; and of those who are assigned to this unfortunate task the physically strongest break the quartz-rock with iron hammers, applying no skill to the task, but only force, and cutting tunnels through the stone, not in a straight line but wherever the seam of gleaming rock may lead.

Now these men, working in darkness as they do because of the bending and winding of the passages, carry lamps bound on their foreheads; and since much of the time they change the position of their bodies to follow the particular character of the stone they throw the blocks, as they cut them out, on the ground; and at this task they labour without ceasing beneath the sternness and blows of an overseer.

Phoenician Trade
Herodotus (c. 440 BC)

This is an interesting description of Phoenician trade with a group in northern Africa.

The Carthaginians say also this, namely, that there is a place in Libya and men dwelling there, outside the Pillars of Heracles,[*] to whom when they have come and have taken the merchandise forth from their ships, they set it in order along the beach and embark again in their ships, and after that they raise a smoke; and the natives of the country seeing the smoke, come to the sea, and then they lay down gold as an equivalent for the merchandise and retire to a distance away from the merchandise.

The Carthaginians upon that disembark and examine it, and if the gold is, in their opinion, sufficient for the value of the merchandise, they take it up and go their way; but if not, they embark again in their ships and sit there; and the others approach and straightway add more gold to the former, until they satisfy them; and they say that neither party wrongs the other; for neither do the Carthaginians lay hands on the gold until it is made equal to the value of their merchandise, nor do the others lay hands on the merchandise until the Carthaginians have taken the gold.

Gold Coin from Carthage (c. 300 BC)

---

[*] *also called the Pillars of Hercules*

Milo of Croton
Pausanias (c. 175 AD)

Pausanias traveled extensively around the Mediterranean in the second century after Christ. His book Description of Greece *details his observations in that country and includes historical anecdotes. In one section, he describes statues of Olympic victors at Olympia. One famous Olympic athlete was Milo of Croton, who lived in the 500s BC. He won 32 wrestling competitions, including six at the Olympic Games. This 1918 translation of Pausanias is by W. H. S. Jones and H. A. Omerod.*

The statue of Milo the son of Diotimus was made by Dameas, also a native of Crotona. Milo won six victories for wrestling at Olympia, one of them among the boys; at Pytho he won six among the men and one among the boys. He came to Olympia to wrestle for the seventh time, but did not succeed in mastering Timasitheus, a fellow-citizen who was also a young man, and who refused, moreover, to come to close quarters with him.

It is further stated that Milo carried his own statue into the Altis. His feats with the pomegranate and the quoit* are also remembered by tradition. He would grasp a pomegranate so firmly that nobody could wrest it from him by force, and yet he did not damage it by pressure. He would stand upon a greased quoit, and make fools of those who charged him and tried to push him from the quoit. He used to perform also the following exhibition feats.

He would tie a cord round his forehead as though it were a ribbon or a crown. Holding his breath and filling with blood the veins on his head, he would break the cord by the strength of these veins. It is said that he would let down by his side his right arm from the shoulder to the elbow, and stretch out straight the arm below the elbow, turning the thumb upwards, while the other fingers lay in a row. In this position, then, the little finger was lowest, but nobody could bend it back by pressure.

---

* *a large flat stone*

A Man's Praise of His Poor Wife
Chinese (c. 680 BC)

James Legge was a Scottish missionary in China from 1840 to 1873. He became the first professor of Chinese at Oxford University from 1876 to 1897. He published numerous translations of Chinese works in English, including a collection of ancient poems. He translated the poems in prose, without rhyme or meter. Helen Waddell was born in Japan to Irish missionary parents and spent the first eleven years of her life there. In 1913 she published her poetic adaptations of Dr. Legge's translations.

I went out at the Eastern Gate,
    I saw the girls in clouds,
Like clouds they were, and soft and bright,
    But in the crowds
I thought on the maid who is my light,
Down-drooping, soft as the grey twilight;
    She is my mate.

I went out by the Tower on the Wall,
    I saw the girls in flower,
Like flowering rushes they swayed and bent,
    But in that hour
I thought on the maid who is my saint,
In her thin white robe and her colouring faint;
    She is my all.

Bronze Basin from This Period in China

Customs of the Persians
Herodotus (c. 450 BC)

This excerpt comes from Book I of The Histories, *translated by George Rawlinson.*

The customs which I know the Persians to observe are the following. They have no images of the gods, no temples nor altars, and consider the use of them a sign of folly. This comes, I think, from their not believing the gods to have the same nature with men, as the Greeks imagine. Their wont, however, is to ascend to the summits of the loftiest mountains and there to offer sacrifice to Zeus,* which is the name they give to the whole circuit of the firmament.

To these gods the Persians offer sacrifice in the following manner: they raise no altar, light no fire, pour no libations; there is no sound of the flute, no putting on of chaplets, no consecrated barley cake; but the man who wishes to sacrifice brings his animal to a spot of ground which is free from pollution, and then calls upon the name of the god to whom he intends to offer.

It is usual to have the turban encircled with a wreath, most commonly of myrtle. The sacrificer is not allowed to pray for blessings on himself alone, but he prays for the welfare of the king and of the whole Persian people, among whom he is of necessity included. He cuts the animal in pieces, and having boiled the flesh, he lays it out upon the tenderest herbage he can find, trefoil especially.

When all is ready, one of the Magi comes forward and chants a hymn, which they say recounts the origin of the gods. It is not lawful to offer a sacrifice unless there is a Magus present. After waiting a short time the sacrificer carries the flesh of the animal away with him, and makes whatever use of it he may please. . . .

When they meet each other in the street, you may know if the persons meeting are of equal rank by the following token: if they are, instead of speaking, they kiss each other on the lips. In the case where one is a little inferior to the other, the kiss is given on the cheek; where the difference of rank is great, the inferior prostrates himself upon the ground.

Of nations, they honor most their nearest neighbors, whom they esteem next to themselves; those who live beyond these they honor in the second degree; and so with the remainder, the further they are removed, the less the esteem in which they hold them. The reason is, that they look upon themselves as very greatly superior in all respects to the rest of mankind, regarding others as approaching in excellence in proportion as they dwell nearer to them; whence it comes to pass that those who are the farthest off must be the most degraded of mankind.

There is no nation which so readily adopts foreign customs as the Persians. Thus, they have taken the dress of the Medes, considering it superior to their own; and in war they wear the Egyptian breastplate. As soon as they hear of any luxury, they instantly make it their own. Each of them has several wives, and a still larger number of concubines.

---

* *Herodotus uses the name of the chief Greek god. The Persians used the name Ahura-Mazda to refer to their deity.*

Next to prowess in arms, it is regarded as the greatest proof of manly excellence, to be the father of many sons. Every year the king sends rich gifts to the man who can show the largest number; for they hold that number is strength. Their sons are carefully instructed from their fifth to their twentieth year, in three things alone—to ride, to draw the bow, and to speak the truth.

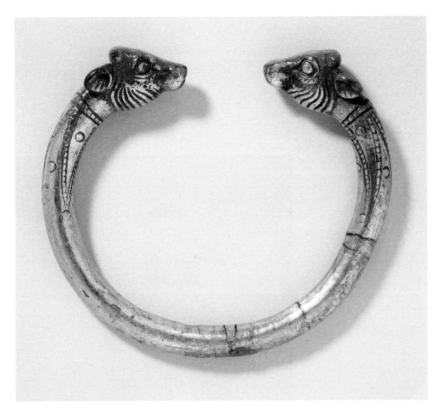

These objects represent personal adornment during this period in ancient Persia. At left is a silver bracelet. At right is a bronze tube for kohl. Kohl is an eye makeup made from minerals. It has been used in many parts of the world for centuries.

The Analects
Confucius (c. 400s BC)

After the death of Confucius (479 BC), his followers wrote down his teachings and put them together in a book known as The Analects. *This book was edited and revised over the centuries. It contains many sayings attributed to Confucius, summarizing his philosophy about how people should live. Here are a few extracts from a translation by James Legge.*

The Master said, "To rule a country of a thousand chariots, there must be reverent attention to business, and sincerity; economy in expenditure, and love for men; and the employment of the people at the proper seasons." (Book I, Chapter 5)

The Master said, "He who exercises government by means of his virtue may be compared to the north polar star, which keeps its place and all the stars turn towards it." (Book II, Chapter 1)

The Master said, "A man should say, 'I am not concerned that I have no place, I am concerned how I may fit myself for one. I am not concerned that I am not known, I seek to be worthy to be known.'" (Book IV, Chapter 14)

The Master said, "When we see men of worth, we should think of equaling them; when we see men of a contrary character, we should turn inwards and examine ourselves." (Book IV, Chapter 17)

The Master said of Tsze-ch'an that he had four of the characteristics of a superior man— in his conduct of himself, he was humble; in serving his superiors, he was respectful; in nourishing the people, he was kind; in ordering the people, he was just. (Book V, Chapter 15)

This illustration of Confucius is from about 1770 AD.

Laws
Plato (c. 360 BC)

Plato's book Laws *contains his ideas about how society should be organized. The book is written in the form of a conversation between three Greek men. This English translation is by Benjamin Jowett.*

"Let us consider a further point. The matters which are now in question are generally called customs rather than laws; and we have already made the reflection that, though they are not, properly speaking, laws, yet neither can they be neglected. For they fill up the interstices of law, and are the props and ligatures on which the strength of the whole building depends. Laws without customs never last; and we must not wonder if habit and custom sometimes lengthen out our laws. . . .

"Up to their third year, then, the life of children may be regulated by customs such as we have described. From three to six their minds have to be amused; but they must not be allowed to become self-willed and spoilt. . . . After six years of age there shall be a separation of the sexes; the boys will go to learn riding and the use of arms, and the girls may, if they please, also learn. Here I note a practical error in early training.

"Mothers and nurses foolishly believe that the left hand is by nature different from the right, whereas the left leg and foot are acknowledged to be the same as the right. But the truth is that nature made all things to balance, and the power of using the left hand, which is of little importance in the case of the plectrum of the lyre, may make a great difference in the art of the warrior, who should be a skilled gymnast and able to fight and balance himself in any position.

"If a man were a Briareus,* he should use all his hundred hands at once; at any rate, let everybody employ the two which they have. To these matters the magistrates, male and female, should attend; the women superintending the nursing and amusement of the children, and the men superintending their education, that all of them, boys and girls alike, may be sound, wind and limb, and not spoil the gifts of nature by bad habits."

This Greek vase depicts a slave handing a child to his mother.

---

* *In Greek mythology, Briareus was the son of Uranus and Gaea. He had fifty heads and one hundred arms and hands.*

Pillars of Ashoka
(c. 250 BC)

Ashoka was an emperor of the Mauryan dynasty in India. He came to power about 50 years after Alexander the Great. He initially used violence to expand his empire, which covered territory that included parts of modern India, Bangladesh, Nepal, Pakistan, and Afghanistan.

Ashoka later advocated nonviolence and religious tolerance. He encouraged the people in his empire to be honest, show compassion, and live simply. Ashoka promoted his ideas through messages inscribed on pillars and rocks throughout his empire. One pillar in modern Afghanistan has inscriptions in the Aramaic and Greek languages, which shows the interaction between different cultural groups at the time.

The lion capital pictured below left originally sat on top of one of Ashoka's pillars at Sarnath, India. It features Buddhist symbolism. The capital became a national emblem of India after it gained independence from the British. The Ashoka Chakra (the wheel below the lions) is featured on the flag of modern India. The pillar at right is a reproduction of this Ashoka pillar, erected in Wat Umong, Thailand, in the 1200s AD.

1 Maccabees
Jewish (c. 100 BC)

The book of 1 Maccabees tells about Judas Maccabeus and the other Jews who fought the Greeks in Israel. 1 Maccabees is one of the books of the Apocrypha, a collection of books written between the time of the Old Testament and the New Testament. Some Christians include these books in their copies of the Bible.

Then Judas his son, who was called Maccabe'us, took command in his place. All his brothers and all who had joined his father helped him; they gladly fought for Israel.

> He extended the glory of his people.
>   Like a giant he put on his breastplate;
> he girded on his armor of war and waged battles,
>   protecting the host by his sword.
> He was like a lion in his deeds,
>   like a lion's cub roaring for prey.
> He searched out and pursued the lawless;
>   he burned those who troubled his people.
> Lawless men shrank back for fear of him;
>   all the evildoers were confounded;
>   and deliverance prospered by his hand.
> He embittered many kings,
>   but he made Jacob glad by his deeds,
>   and his memory is blessed for ever.
> He went through the cities of Judah;
>   he destroyed the ungodly out of the land;
>   thus he turned away wrath from Israel.
> He was renowned to the ends of the earth;
>   he gathered in those who were perishing.

But Apollo'nius gathered together Gentiles and a large force from Samar'ia to fight against Israel. When Judas learned of it, he went out to meet him, and he defeated and killed him. Many were wounded and fell, and the rest fled. Then they seized their spoils; and Judas took the sword of Apollo'nius, and used it in battle the rest of his life.

Now when Seron, the commander of the Syrian army, heard that Judas had gathered a large company, including a body of faithful men who stayed with him and went out to battle, he said, "I will make a name for myself and win honor in the kingdom. I will make war on Judas and his companions, who scorn the king's command." And again a strong army of ungodly men went up with him to help him, to take vengeance on the sons of Israel.

When he approached the ascent of Beth-hor'on, Judas went out to meet him with a small company. But when they saw the army coming to meet them, they said to Judas, "How can we, few as we are, fight against so great and strong a multitude? And we are faint, for we have eaten nothing today." Judas replied, "It is easy for many to be hemmed in by few, for in the sight of Heaven there is no difference between saving by many or by few. It is not on the size of the army that victory in battle depends, but strength comes from Heaven. They come against us in great pride and lawlessness to destroy us and our wives and our children, and to despoil us; but we fight for our lives and our laws. He himself will crush them before us; as for you, do not be afraid of them."

When he finished speaking, he rushed suddenly against Seron and his army, and they were crushed before him. They pursued them down the descent of Beth-hor'on to the plain; eight hundred of them fell, and the rest fled into the land of the Philistines. Then Judas and his brothers began to be feared, and terror fell upon the Gentiles round about them. His fame reached the king, and the Gentiles talked of the battles of Judas.

Judas Maccabeus Pursues Timotheus, *Gustave Doré (French, 1866)*

Homeschooling in Ancient Rome
Plutarch (c. 76 AD)

Marcus Cato, or Cato the Elder, lived from 234 to 149 BC. He was a government official and author. He wrote a book on the history of Rome and another on farming practices. Plutarch (c. 46-120 AD) was a Greek author who became a Roman citizen. He compiled a series of biographies called Lives of the Noble Greeks and Romans. *This excerpt from Plutarch's biography of Cato the Elder describes how Cato homeschooled his son.*

As soon as the boy showed signs of understanding, his father took him under his own charge and taught him to read, although he had an accomplished slave, Chilo by name, who was a school-teacher, and taught many boys. Still, Cato thought it not right, as he tells us himself, that his son should be scolded by a slave, or have his ears tweaked when he was slow to learn, still less that he should be indebted to his slave for such a priceless thing as education.

He was therefore himself not only the boys' reading-teacher, but his tutor in law, and his athletic trainer, and he taught his son not merely to hurl the javelin and fight in armour and ride the horse, but also to box, to endure heat and cold, and to swim lustily through the eddies and billows of the Tiber.

His *History of Rome*, as he tells us himself, he wrote out with his own hand and in large characters, that his son might have in his own home an aid to acquaintance with his country's ancient traditions.

Description of Julius Caesar
Suetonius (121 AD)

Suetonius, a Roman government official, compiled biographies of the Roman Emperors from Julius Caesar to Domitian. These excerpts about Julius Caesar are from a translation by Alexander Thomson and T. Forester, published as The Lives of the Twelve Caesars.

It is said that he was tall, of a fair complexion, round limbed, rather full faced, with eyes black and piercing; and that he enjoyed excellent health, except towards the close of his life, when he was subject to sudden fainting-fits, and disturbance in his sleep. He was likewise twice seized with the falling sickness while engaged in active service.

He was nice in the care of his person and kept the hair of his head closely cut and had his face smoothly shaved. His baldness gave him much uneasiness, having often found himself upon that account exposed to the jibes of his enemies. He therefore used to bring forward the hair from the crown of his head; and of all the honours conferred upon him by the senate and people, there was none which he either accepted or used with greater pleasure, than the right of wearing constantly a laurel crown.

It is said that he was particular in his dress. For he used the Latus Clavus with fringes about the wrists, and always had it girded about him, but rather loosely.* This circumstance gave origin to the expression of Sylla, who often advised the nobles to beware of "the ill-girt boy."

He was perfect in the use of arms, an accomplished rider, and able to endure fatigue beyond all belief. On a march, he used to go at the head of his troops, sometimes on horseback, but oftener on foot, with his head bare in all kinds of weather. He would travel post in a light carriage without baggage, at the rate of a hundred miles a day; and if he was stopped by floods in the rivers, he swam across, or floated on skins inflated with wind, so that he often anticipated intelligence of his movements.

The Latus Clavus was a broad stripe of purple, on the front of the toga. Its width distinguished it from that of the soldiers, who wore it narrow.

O Sing a Song of Bethlehem
Louis F. Benson (1899)

Louis Benson (1855-1930) was a Presbyterian minister who studied the history and use of hymns in churches. He collected 9,000 hymnals and related books. He also composed hymns, such as this one, which he published in The School Hymnal.

O sing a song of Bethlehem, of shepherds watching there,
And of the news that came to them from angels in the air.
The light that shone on Bethlehem fills all the world today;
Of Jesus' birth and peace on earth the angels sing alway.

O sing a song of Nazareth, of sunny days of joy;
O sing of fragrant flowers' breath, and of the sinless Boy.
For now the flowers of Nazareth in every heart may grow;
Now spreads the fame of His dear name on all the winds that blow.

O sing a song of Galilee, of lake and woods and hill,
Of Him who walked upon the sea and bade the waves be still.
For though like waves on Galilee, dark seas of trouble roll,
When faith has heard the Master's Word, falls peace upon the soul.

O sing a song of Calvary, its glory and dismay,
Of Him who hung upon the tree, and took our sins away.
For He who died on Calvary is risen from the grave,
And Christ, our Lord, by Heaven adored, is mighty now to save.

Modern Nazareth in the Beit Netofa Valley of Galilee

There is a Sea
Lula Klingman Zahn (1921)

This hymn portrays the contrast between the Sea of Galilee and the Dead Sea. The first verse is about the Sea of Galilee, the "stream more wide" is the Jordan River, and the second verse is about the Dead Sea. The third verse asks whether we will be people who give what we receive to bless others or people who cling to our gifts only for ourselves. In living the first way, we follow the example of Jesus. The first two verses are of uncertain origin, the third verse and tune were written by Mrs. Zahn.

There is a sea which day by day receives the rippling rills,
And streams that spring from wells of God, or fall from cedared hills.
But what it thus receives it gives with glad unsparing hand;
A stream more wide, with deeper tide, flows on to lower land.

There is a sea which day by day receives a fuller tide;
But all its store it keeps, nor gives to shore nor sea beside.
Its Jordan's stream, now turned to brine, lies heavy as molten lead;
Its dreadful name doth e'er proclaim that sea is waste and dead.

Which shall it be for you and me, who God's good gifts obtain?
Shall we accept for self alone, or take to give again?
For He who once was rich indeed laid all His glory down,
That by His grace our ransomed race should share His wealth and crown.

The Roman Roads

J. R. S. Sterrett (1899)

This description of the Roman roads was published in The Nation *magazine. Author J. R. S. Sterrett was an American scholar and archaeologist.*

The width of the Roman road varied much according to its importance. Often it was one hundred and twenty feet wide, though in the provinces it was generally sixty, sometimes forty feet wide. In order to understand the reason for this great width and for the substantial construction that was rigidly adhered to, we should bear in mind the make-up of the Roman army, whose comfort and necessities were continually consulted.

In the first place, the Roman soldier was burdened by his heavy armor and other impedimenta in such a manner as to render him wholly unfit to repel sudden attacks successfully, as we read on nearly every page of Caesar's *Commentaries*. The baggage-train was far larger and more unwieldy than anything we know of to-day, for the reason that this train had to transport not merely the tents, artillery, arms, munitions of war, army chests, and a host of other things necessary in the warfare of that day; not merely the effects and plunder of the legionaries, but also those of two secondary armies—an army of women, wives of the legionaries and camp-followers, and another army of body-servants, for each legionary had one or more servants, so that the *calones** outnumbered the legionaries themselves.

When on the march this unwieldy army maintained the line-of-battle order, theoretically at least, in order to be ready to repel sudden and unexpected attack. Good roads, therefore, were necessary in order to enable the immense train with which the army was handicapped to keep pace with the legionaries, and wide roads were essential, in order, in case of sudden attack, to allow the individual legionaries to make effective use of their arms without interfering with their neighbors.

The Roman roads were built with more care than is expended upon the beds of our railways even. They were made as straight as possible, and natural obstacles were skillfully overcome by the use of cuts, fills, bridges, culverts, embankments, and even tunnels. Stiff grades were avoided, and a level, once reached, was doggedly maintained, even at the expense of making cuts, fills, etc. The work preliminary to the building of any Roman road consisted in excavating all the dirt down to hardpan, and the excavation thus made was filled in, regardless of expense, with layers of sand, stone, and cement, until the requisite level, however high it might be, had been reached. Finally, the surface was dressed with a layer of metal and cement.

The road was practically indestructible, and required only occasional repairs. That continuous or even merely yearly repairs were not necessary seems clear from the fact that, when repairs were made, the propraetor of the province thought it so important an event that he celebrated it by inscribing the fact along with his name on the milestones.

---

* *Servants of the Roman soldiers.*

Many years ago Bergier made an examination of certain Roman roads still in use in France. One road was examined at a point where it had been raised twenty feet above the level of the surrounding country, and a vertical section revealed a structure of five layers. First came the great fill of sixteen feet and one half; on the top of this fill were layers of flattish stones mixed with cement, flattish stones without cement, firmly packed dirt, small metal in hard cement, and large metal and cement, five layers in all, the first three of twelve inches each, the last two of six inches each. Other roads investigated by Bergier, while differing in treatment, were just as substantial roads. Paved roads were rare, but the Via Appia offers a remarkable instance of a paved road. The stone used in its pavement is of the kind of which millstones are made, and they are so carefully dressed and adjusted that the road often seems to be solid rock, and has proved so indestructible that, after two thousand years of continuous use, it is still a superb road.

The Eruption of Mount Vesuvius
Pliny the Younger (c. 107)

Pliny the Elder (23-79 AD) was a soldier and scholar. He died during the eruption of Vesuvius. Pliny's nephew, known as Pliny the Younger, wrote to the Roman historian Tacitus about the event. This excerpt is from the translation by William Melmoth, revised by F. C. T. Bosanquet, and published in The Letters of Pliny *(1909).*

A panic-stricken crowd followed us, and (as to a mind distracted with terror every suggestion seems more prudent than its own) pressed on us in dense array to drive us forward as we came out. Being at a convenient distance from the houses, we stood still, in the midst of a most dangerous and dreadful scene. The chariots, which we had ordered to be drawn out, were so agitated backwards and forwards, though upon the most level ground, that we could not keep them steady, even by supporting them with large stones. The sea seemed to roll back upon itself, and to be driven from its banks by the convulsive motion of the earth; it is certain at least the shore was considerably enlarged, and several sea animals were left upon it.

Destruction of Pompeii and Herculaneum, *John Martin (English, 1821)*

continued

On the other side, a black and dreadful cloud, broken with rapid, zigzag flashes, revealed behind it variously shaped masses of flame: these last were like sheet-lightning, but much larger. Upon this our Spanish friend, whom I mentioned above, addressing himself to my mother and me with great energy and urgency: "If your brother," he said, "if your uncle be safe, he certainly wishes you may be so too; but if he perished, it was his desire, no doubt, that you might both survive him: why therefore do you delay your escape a moment?" . . .

The ashes now began to fall upon us, though in no great quantity. I looked back; a dense dark mist seemed to be following us, spreading itself over the country like a cloud. "Let us turn out of the high-road," I said, "while we can still see, for fear that, should we fall in the road, we should be pressed to death in the dark, by the crowds that are following us." We had scarcely sat down when night came upon us, not such as we have when the sky is cloudy, or when there is no moon, but that of a room when it is shut up, and all the lights put out. . . .

At last this dreadful darkness was dissipated by degrees, like a cloud or smoke; the real day returned, and even the sun shone out, though with a lurid light, like when an eclipse is coming on. Every object that presented itself to our eyes (which were extremely weakened) seemed changed, being covered deep with ashes as if with snow. We returned to Misenum, where we refreshed ourselves as well as we could, and passed an anxious night between hope and fear; though, indeed, with a much larger share of the latter: for the earthquake still continued, while many frenzied persons ran up and down heightening their own and their friends' calamities by terrible predictions.

Mount Vesuvius is seen behind these excavated ruins from Pompeii.

Josephus and the Jews
Josephus (c. 100)

Josephus was born a few years after Jesus went back to heaven. He grew up in Jerusalem. As a young man, he explored the major Jewish schools of thought. This excerpt from his autobiography was translated by William Whiston.

Now, my father Matthias was not only eminent on account of his nobility, but had a higher commendation on account of his righteousness, and was in great reputation in Jerusalem, the greatest city we have. I was myself brought up with my brother, whose name was Matthias, for he was my own brother, by both father and mother; and I made mighty proficiency in the improvements of my learning, and appeared to have both a great memory and understanding.

Moreover, when I was a child, and about fourteen years of age, I was commended by all for the love I had to learning; on which account the high priests and principal men of the city came then frequently to me together, in order to know my opinion about the accurate understanding of points of the law. And when I was about sixteen years old, I had a mind to make trim of the several sects that were among us.

These sects are three: The first is that of the Pharisees, the second that of the Sadducees, and the third that of the Essenes, as we have frequently told you; for I thought that by this means I might choose the best, if I were once acquainted with them all; so I contented myself with

Statue of Josephus at the Masada Fortress Museum

hard fare, and underwent great difficulties, and went through them all. Nor did I content myself with these trials only; but when I was informed that one, whose name was Banus, lived in the desert, and used no other clothing than grew upon trees, and had no other food than what grew of its own accord, and bathed himself in cold water frequently, both by night and by day, in order to preserve his chastity, I imitated him in those things, and continued with him three years.

So when I had accomplished my desires, I returned back to the city, being now nineteen years old, and began to conduct myself according to the rules of the sect of the Pharisees, which is of kin to the sect of the Stoics, as the Greeks call them.

Letter to Calvisius
Pliny the Younger (c. 100)

Roman chariot races involved competition between four major companies or teams: Red, White, Blue, and Green. The members of each team wore tunics of that color. At the races, fans of each color would cheer for their team. Sometimes fights broke out between fans of opposing teams. This letter from Pliny the Younger explains his lack of interest in the competitions.

I have spent these several days past, in reading and writing, with the most pleasing tranquillity imaginable. You will ask, "How that can possibly be in the midst of Rome?"

It was the time of celebrating the Circensian games; an entertainment for which I have not the least taste. They have no novelty, no variety to recommend them, nothing, in short, one would wish to see twice. It does the more surprise me therefore that so many thousand people should be possessed with the childish passion of desiring so often to see a parcel of horses gallop, and men standing upright in their chariots.

If, indeed, it were the swiftness of the horses, or the skill of the men that attracted them, there might be some pretence of reason for it. But it is the uniforms they like; it is the uniform that takes their fancy. And if, in the midst of the course and contest, the different parties were to change colours, their different partisans would change sides, and instantly desert the very same men and horses whom just before they were eagerly following with their eyes, as far as they could see, and shouting out their names with all their might.

Such mighty charms, such wondrous power reside in the colour of a paltry tunic! And this not only with the common crowd (more contemptible than the dress they espouse), but even with serious-thinking people. When I observe such men thus insatiably fond of so silly, so low, so uninteresting, so common an entertainment, I congratulate myself on my indifference to these pleasures: and am glad to employ the leisure of this season upon my books, which others throw away upon the most idle occupations. Farewell.

Roman Chariot Reenactor at Jerash, Jordan

The Martyrdom of Perpetua

(c. 203)

Persecution against Christians continued for decades in the Roman Empire after the death of Polycarp. Perpetua was a young mother about twenty-two years old from the African town of Carthage. She and several other Christians, including a woman named Felicitas, were arrested and condemned to die because of their faith.

Perpetua's mother and brothers were also Christians, but her father was not. He tried several times to persuade her to abandon her faith. The jailer in charge of Perpetua allowed her to receive visitors and to record her experiences. This excerpt is from her journal, as translated by R.E. Wallis in the Ante-Nicene Fathers, Volume 3 *(1885).*

While we were still with the persecutors, and my father, for the sake of his affection for me, was persisting in seeking to turn me away, and to cast me down from the faith—

"Father," said I, "do you see, let us say, this vessel lying here to be a little pitcher, or something else?"

And he said, "I see it to be so."

And I replied to him, "Can it be called by any other name than what it is?"

And he said, "No."

"Neither can I call myself anything else than what I am, a Christian." . . .

After a few days we are taken into the dungeon, and I was very much afraid, because I had never felt such darkness. O terrible day! O the fierce heat of the shock of the soldiery, because of the crowds! . . .

And then my father came to me from the city, worn out with anxiety. . . . And I grieved over the grey hairs of my father, that he alone of all my family would not rejoice over my passion. And I comforted him, saying, "On that scaffold whatever God wills shall happen. For know that we are not placed in our own power, but in that of God."

Perpetua and Felicitas were soon after killed in the arena. This mosaic depicting Perpetua is from a church in Croatia.

Nicene Creed

(325)

This is an English translation of the original Nicene Creed from Philip Schaff's 1876 book Creeds of Christendom.

We believe in one God, the Father Almighty,
  Maker of all things visible and invisible.

And in one Lord Jesus Christ, the Son of God, begotten of the Father, the only-begotten;
    that is, of the essence of the Father, God of God, Light of Light,
    very God of very God, begotten, not made, being of one substance with the Father;
  By whom all things were made both in heaven and on earth;
  Who for us men, and for our salvation, came down
    and was incarnate and was made man;
  He suffered, and the third day he rose again, ascended into heaven;
    from thence He shall come to judge the quick and the dead.

And in the Holy Ghost.

Letter to Laeta
Jerome (403)

Toxotius and Laeta had a little girl named Paula. Jerome was a church leader in Bethlehem. Laeta wrote to Jerome asking for his advice on how to educate Paula. This is part of his response. Paula later lived in Bethlehem.

Thus must a soul be trained which is to be a temple of God. It must learn to hear nothing and to say nothing save what pertains to the fear of the Lord. It must have no comprehension of foul words, no knowledge of worldly songs, and its childish tongue must be imbued with the sweet music of the psalms. Let boys with their wanton frolics be kept far from Paula: let even her maids and attendants hold aloof from association with the worldly, lest they render their evil knowledge worse by teaching it to her.

Have a set of letters made for her, of boxwood or of ivory, and tell her their names. Let her play with them, making play a road to learning, and let her not only grasp the right order of the letters and remember their names in a simple song, but also frequently upset their order and mix the last letters with the middle ones, the middle with the first. Thus she will know them all by sight as well as by sound.

When she begins with uncertain hand to use the pen, either let another hand be put over hers to guide her baby fingers, or else have the letters marked on the tablet so that her writing may follow their outlines and keep to their limits without straying away. Offer her prizes for spelling, tempting her with such trifling gifts as please young children. Let her have companions too in her lessons, so that she may seek to rival them and be stimulated by any praise they win. You must not scold her if she is somewhat slow; praise is the best sharpener of wits. Let her be glad when she is first and sorry when she falls behind. Above all take care not to make her lessons distasteful; a childish dislike often lasts longer than childhood.

The very words from which she will get into the way of forming sentences should not be taken at haphazard but be definitely chosen and arranged on purpose. For example, let her have the names of the prophets and the apostles, and the whole list of patriarchs from Adam downwards, as Matthew and Luke give it. She will then be doing two things at the same time, and will remember them afterwards.

Statue of Jerome at the Church of the Nativity in Bethlehem

A Visit with Attila

Priscus (c. 450)

Priscus was a diplomat sent from the Eastern Roman Empire to meet with Attila the Hun in 448. This excerpt from Priscus' description of that visit was included in Readings in European History *by James Harvey Robinson (1904).*

I saw a number of people advancing, and a great commotion and noise, Attila's egress being expected. And he came forth from the house with a dignified strut, looking round on this side and on that. He was accompanied by Onegesius,* and stood in front of the house; and many persons who had lawsuits with one another came up and received his judgment. Then he returned into the house and received ambassadors of barbarous peoples. . . .

When the hour arrived [for a banquet] we went to the palace, along with the embassy from the western Romans, and stood on the threshold of the hall in the presence of Attila. The cupbearers gave us a cup, according to the national custom, that we might pray before we sat down. Having tasted the cup, we proceeded to take our seats, all the chairs being ranged along the walls of the room on either side.

Attila sat in the middle on a couch; a second couch was set behind him, and from it steps led up to his bed, which was covered with linen sheets and wrought coverlets for ornament, such as Greeks and Romans used to deck bridal beds. The places on the right of Attila were held chief in honor; those on the left, where we sat, were only second. . . .

The attendant of Attila first entered with a dish full of meat, and behind him came the other attendants with bread and viands,** which they laid on the tables. A luxurious meal, served on silver plate, had been made ready for us and the barbarian guests, but Attila ate nothing but meat on a wooden trencher. In everything else, too, he showed himself temperate; his cup was of wood, while to the guests were given goblets of gold and silver. His dress, too, was quite simple, affecting only to be clean. The sword he carried at his side, the latchets of his Scythian*** shoes, the bridle of his horse were not adorned, like those of the other Scythians, with gold or gems or anything costly.

When the viands of the first course had been consumed, we all stood up, and did not resume our seats until each one, in the order before observed, drank to the health of Attila in the goblet of wine presented to him. We then sat down, and a second dish was placed on each table with eatables of another kind. After this course the same ceremony was observed as after the first. When evening fell torches were lit, and two barbarians coming forward in front of Attila sang songs they had composed, celebrating his victories and deeds of valor in war.

One of Attila's chiefs
**Food*
***Scythian is the name the Greeks had used for the nomads of Central Asia*

The Deer's Cry

Irish

Also known as St. Patrick's Lorica (or Breastplate), this poem has traditionally been attributed to Patrick, though the current version was likely revised later. Regardless of its exact origin, it shows the influence of Christianity in Ireland. This version is taken from Selections from Ancient Irish Poetry, *translated by Kuno Meyer, and published in 1911.*

I arise to-day
Through a mighty strength,
   the invocation of the Trinity,
Through belief in the threeness,
Through confession of the oneness
Of the Creator of Creation.

I arise to-day
Through the strength of Christ's birth
   with His baptism,
Through the strength of His crucifixion
   with His burial,
Through the strength of His resurrection
   with His ascension,
Through the strength of His descent
   for the judgment of Doom.

I arise to-day
Through the strength of
   the love of Cherubim,
In obedience of angels,
In the service of archangels,
In hope of resurrection
   to meet with reward,
In prayers of patriarchs,
In predictions of prophets,
In preachings of apostles,
In faiths of confessors,
In innocence of holy virgins,
In deeds of righteous men.

I arise to-day
Through the strength of heaven:
Light of sun,
Radiance of moon,
Splendour of fire,
Speed of lightning,
Swiftness of wind,
Depth of sea,
Stability of earth,
Firmness of rock.

I arise to day
Through God's strength to pilot me:
God's might to uphold me,
God's wisdom to guide me,
God's eye to look before me,
God's ear to hear me,
God's word to speak for me,
God's hand to guard me,
God's way to lie before me,
God's shield to protect me,
God's host to save me
From snares of devils,
From temptations of vices,
From every one who shall wish me ill,
Afar and anear,
Alone and in a multitude.

continued

I summon to-day all these powers
    between me and those evils,
Against every cruel merciless power
    that may oppose my body and soul,
Against incantations of false prophets,
Against black laws of pagandom,
Against false laws of heretics,
Against craft of idolatry,
Against spells of women and smiths
    and wizards,
Against every knowledge that corrupts
    man's body and soul.

Christ to shield me to-day
Against poison, against burning,
Against drowning, against wounding,
So that there may come to me
    abundance of reward.
Christ with me, Christ before me,
    Christ behind me,
Christ in me, Christ beneath me,
    Christ above me,
Christ on my right, Christ on my left,
Christ when I lie down, Christ when
    I sit down, Christ when I arise,
Christ in the heart of every man who
    thinks of me,
Christ in the mouth of every one who
    speaks of me,
Christ in every eye that sees me,
Christ in every ear that hears me.

I arise to-day
Through a mighty strength,
    the invocation of the Trinity,
Through belief in the threeness,
Through confession of the oneness
Of the Creator of Creation.

Celtic Cross in Ireland

Japanese Poems
(600s-700s)

In 1235 Sadaiye Fujiwara collected one hundred Japanese poems written over several centuries into the Hyaku-nin-isshiu. *These approximate translations by William Porter were published in* A Hundred Verses from Old Japan *(1909).*

Out in the fields this autumn day
　　They're busy reaping grain;
I sought for shelter 'neath this roof,
　　But fear I sought in vain,—
　　My sleeve is wet with rain.
　　　　—Emperor Tenchi (c. 670)

The spring has gone, the summer's come,
　　And I can just descry
The peak of Ama-no-kagu,
　　Where angels of the sky
　　Spread their white robes to dry.
　　　　—Empress Jito (c. 695)

Long is the mountain pheasant's tail
　　That curves down in its flight;
But longer still, it seems to me,
　　Left in my lonely plight,
　　Is this unending night.
　　　　—Kaki-no-Moto (c. 700)

I started off along the shore,
　　The sea shore at Tago,
And saw the white and glist'ning peak
　　Of Fuji all aglow
　　Through falling flakes of snow.
　　　　—Akahito Yamabe (c. 700)

While gazing up into the sky,
　　My thoughts have wandered far;
Methinks I see the rising moon
　　Above Mount Mikasa
　　At far-off Kasuga.
　　　　—Nakamaro Abe (c. 726)

Garden in Autumn, Kyoto, Japan

Al Mansur, Builder of Baghdad, and the Poet
Arabic (700s)

This eighth-century story was adapted from the Arabic by Claude Field and published in The World's Story: A History of the World in Story, Song and Art, Volume 3 (1914).

Al Mansur, the third caliph of the House of Abbas, succeeded his brother Es-Saffah AD 754. He was a prince of great prudence, integrity, and discretion; but these good qualities were sullied by his extraordinary covetousness and occasional cruelty.

He patronized poets and learned men, and was endowed with a remarkable memory. It is said that he could remember a poem after having only once heard it. He also had a slave who could commit to memory anything that he had heard twice, and a slave-girl who could do the same with what she had heard three times.

One day there came to him a poet bringing a congratulatory ode, and Al Mansur said to him: "If it appears that anybody knows it by heart, or that any one composed it,—that is to say, that it was brought here by some other person before thee,—we will give thee no recompense for it; but if no one knows it, we will give thee the weight in money of that upon which it is written."

So the poet repeated his poem, and the caliph at once committed it to memory, although it contained a thousand lines. Then he said to the poet: "Listen to it from me," and he recited it perfectly. Then he added: "And this slave, too, knows it by heart." This was the case, as he had heard it twice, once from the poet and once from the caliph. Then the caliph said: "And this slave-girl, who is concealed by the curtain, she also recollects it." So she repeated every letter of it, and the poet went away unrewarded.

Another poet, El Asmaiy, was among the intimate friends and table companions of the caliph. He composed some very difficult verses, and scratched them upon a fragment of a marble pillar, which he wrapped in a cloak and placed on the back of a camel. Then he disguised himself like a foreign Arab, and fastened on a face-cloth, so that nothing was visible but his eyes, and came to the caliph and said: "Verily I have lauded the Commander of the Faithful in a 'Kasidah'" (ode).

Then said Al Mansur: "O brother of the Arabs! if the poem has been brought by any one beside thee, we will give thee no recompense for it; otherwise we will bestow on thee the weight in money of that upon which it is written."

So El Asmaiy recited the "Kasidah," which, as it was extraordinarily intricate and difficult, the caliph could not commit to memory. He looked toward the slave and the girl, but they had neither of them learnt it. So he cried: "O brother of the Arabs! Bring hither that whereon it is written, that we may give thee its weight."

Then said the seeming Arab: "O my Lord! of a truth I could find no paper to write it upon; but I had amongst the things left me at my father's death a piece of a marble column which had been thrown aside as useless, so I scratched the 'Kasidah' upon that."

Then the caliph had no help for it but to give him its weight in gold, and this nearly exhausted his treasury. The poet took it and departed.

Patolli Board Game
Mesoamerican

Diego Durán was born in Spain in 1537 but moved to Mexico as a boy. He compiled an extensive historical account and a series of illustrations of Aztec history and culture. One of his illustrations, shown below from a 19th-century Mexican reprint, depicts the game of patolli. Archeological and historical evidence suggests that the Maya played a similar game hundreds of years earlier, during the time Palenque was growing.

The exact rules for playing patolli are unclear, and different people groups probably played variations of the game. Players evidently threw marked beans like dice. Then they moved their pieces around the board and attempted to remove opposing pieces. Patolli has some similarities to the Asian Indian game of pachisi, but the two games probably developed independently from each other.

Illustration of the Game Patolli

The Tooth Thrall
Scandinavian

The Vikings passed down stories about their ancestors called sagas. Some of these sagas were written down. Jennie Hall was a teacher at Frances W. Parker School in Chicago. She adapted some of these stories and compiled them in the 1902 book Viking Tales. *The boy in the story, Harald, was the son of Halfdan. According to later Viking tradition, Harald became the first king of Norway.*

The Vikings captured prisoners during their raids all over Europe. These captives became slaves and were called thralls. Thor is the name of a pagan god in Norse mythology who carries a hammer.

When Harald was seven months old he cut his first tooth. Then his father said:

"All the young of my herds, lambs and calves and colts, that have been born since this baby was born I this day give to him. I also give to him this thrall, Olaf. These are my tooth-gifts to my son."

The boy grew fast, for as soon as he could walk about he was out of doors most of the time. He ran in the woods and climbed the hills and waded in the creek. He was much with his tooth thrall, for the king had said to Olaf: "Be ever at his call."

Now this Olaf was full of stories, and Harald liked to hear them. "Come out to Aegir's Rock, Olaf, and tell me stories," he said almost every day.

So they started off across the hills. The man wore a long, loose coat of white wool, belted at the waist with a strap. He had on coarse shoes and leather leggings. Around his neck was an iron collar welded together so that it could not come off. On it were strange marks, called runes, that said: "Olaf, thrall of Halfdan."

But Harald's clothes were gay. A cape of gray velvet hung from his shoulders. It was fastened over his breast with great gold buckles. When it waved in the wind, a scarlet lining flashed out, and the bottom of a little scarlet jacket showed. His feet and legs were covered with gray woolen tights. Gold lacings wound around his legs from his shoes to his knees. A band of gold held down his long, yellow hair.

It was a wild country that these two were walking over. They were climbing steep, rough hills. Some of them seemed made all of rock, with a little earth lying in spots. Great rocks hung out from them, with trees growing in their cracks. Some big pieces had broken off and rolled down the hill.

"Thor broke them," Olaf said. "He rides through the sky and hurls his hammer at clouds and at mountains. That makes the thunder and the lightning and cracks the hills. His hammer never misses its aim, and it always comes back to his hand and is eager to go again."

When they reached the top of the hill they looked back. Far below was a soft, green valley. In front of it the sea came up into the land and made a fjord. On each side of the fjord high walls of rock stood up and made the water black with shadow. All around the valley were high hills with dark pines on them. Far off were the mountains. In the valley were Halfdan's houses around their square yard.

"How little our houses look down there!" Harald said. "But I can almost—yes, I can see the red dragon on the roof of the feast hall. Do you remember when I climbed up and sat on his head, Olaf?" He laughed and kicked his heels and ran on.

At last they came to Aegir's Rock and walked up on its flat top. Harald went to the edge and looked over. A ragged wall of rock reached down, and two hundred feet below was the black water of the fjord. Olaf watched him for a while, then he said: "No whitening of your cheek, Harald? Good! A boy that can face the fall of Aegir's Rock will not be afraid to face the war flash when he is a man."

Illustration from Viking Tales

Ukrainian Folk Songs

Sometimes when the gospel spreads in a nation, people who want to follow Christ also hold on to traditional beliefs and practices. Hundreds of years ago, the Slavic people of modern Ukraine believed that Vesnianka was a young female goddess who represented the coming of spring. These two songs reflect that belief. They were translated by Florence Randal Livesay and published in 1916.

Vesnianka,
A Children's Song

Vesnianka came,
And brought Paradise.
All is blooming, everywhere.
Beauty in the meadows lies,
Joy is in the fields and air,
In the woods is Song.

Let us garlands make
On Vesnianka's Day.
Join hands, and in a ring
Interweaving, let us play
Jumping high, the while we sing
    In the woods our Song!

All of beauty, life,
Goes when winter's here.
Bloom will perish, birds grow dumb,
All things lovely disappear.
But the time has not yet come
    To leave off our Song.

Hyeevka,
A Song of the Woods

What did she bring us, the beautiful Spring?
Fair tresses, maiden's beauty.
A maiden's beauty is as dew in summer
Washed in a spring, dried in an oven,
Set on a table, wrapped in paper.

Springtime! And now what is it she brings us?
She brought us Strength, beauty of boys.
Beauty of boys is as dew in summer
Washed in a rain-pond, dried on a fence,
Set on a table, wrapped in rags.

After the coming of Christianity, the custom developed of modifying the traditional songs and dances to celebrate the coming of spring and the resurrection of Jesus. Ukrainians still perform these songs and dances in the spring. They are known as vesnianky or hahilky.

The Life of King Alfred

Asser (c. 893)

Asser was a scholar who worked closely with King Alfred, and Asser composed a biography of the king during the 890s. The only surviving complete manuscript of the biography was destroyed in a fire, but it has been reconstructed from other copies. This excerpt is from a translation by J. A. Giles, published in 1847.

He was loved by his father and mother, and even by all the people, above all his brothers, and was educated altogether at the court of the king. As he advanced through the years of infancy and youth, his form appeared more comely than that of his brothers; in look, in speech, and in manners he was more graceful than they. His noble nature implanted in him from his cradle a love of wisdom above all things; but, with shame be it spoken, by the unworthy neglect of his parents and nurses, he remained illiterate even till he was twelve years old or more; but, he listened with serious attention to the Saxon poems which he often heard recited, and easily retained them in his docile memory. He was a zealous practiser of hunting in all its branches, and hunted with great assiduity and success; for skill and good fortune in this art, as in all others, are among the gifts of God, as we also have often witnessed.

On a certain day, therefore, his mother was showing him and his brothers a Saxon book of poetry, which she held in her hand, and said, "Whichever of you shall the soonest learn this volume shall have it for his own." Stimulated by these words, or rather by the Divine inspiration, and allured by the beautifully illuminated letter at the beginning of the volume, he spoke before all his brothers, who, though his seniors in age, were not so in grace, and answered, "Will you really give that book to one of us, that is to say, to him who can first understand and repeat it to you?" At this his mother smiled with satisfaction, and confirmed what she had before said. Upon which the boy took the book out of her hand, and went to his master to read it, and in due time brought it to his mother and recited it.

After this he learned the daily course, that is, the celebration of the hours, and afterwards certain psalms, and several prayers, contained in a certain book which he kept day and night in his bosom, as we ourselves have seen, and carried about with him to assist his prayers, amid all the bustle and business of this present life. But, sad to say, he could not gratify his most ardent wish to learn the liberal arts, because, as he said, there were no good readers at that time in all the kingdom of the West-Saxons.

continued

This he confessed, with many lamentations and sighs, to have been one of his greatest difficulties and impediments in this life, namely, that when he was young and had the capacity for learning, he could not find teachers; but, when he was more advanced in life, he was harassed by so many diseases unknown to all the physicians of this island, as well as by internal and external anxieties of sovereignty, and by continual invasions of the pagans, and had his teachers and writers also so much disturbed, that there was no time for reading. But yet among the impediments of this present life, from infancy up to the present time, and, as I believe, even until his death, he continued to feel the same insatiable desire of knowledge, and still aspires after it.

During his reign, Alfred was a strong promoter of education in England. He oversaw the translation of several books from Latin into English and did some of the translation work himself. One of the books he translated was Pastoral Care, *written by Pope Gregory I (540-604). Alfred distributed copies of this book to bishops in England. The jewel pictured below is apparently one of several that were designed during Alfred's reign. The text around the edge of the jewel reads: "Alfred had me made." One jewel evidently accompanied each copy of* Pastoral Care, *being attached to a rod and used as a pointer while reading.*

The Alexiad
Anna Comnena (c. 1148)

Anna Comnena (1083-1153) was the daughter of the Byzantine Emperor Alexius I and his wife Irene Doukaina. The oldest of seven children, she received an excellent education and became a scholar and a physician. Anna's husband Nikephoros began writing an historical account that focused on Anna's father Alexius. After Nikephoros died, Anna continued his research and published a fifteen-volume account of Byzantine history during her father's reign. It includes many details about the First Crusade. This excerpt is from the translation by Elizabeth A. S. Dawes.

Time in its irresistible and ceaseless flow carries along on its flood all created things, and drowns them in the depths of obscurity, no matter if they be quite unworthy of mention, or most noteworthy and important, and thus, as the tragedian says, "he brings from the darkness all things to the birth, and all things born envelops in the night."[*]

But the tale of history forms a very strong bulwark against the stream of time, and to some extent checks its irresistible flow, and, of all things done in it, as many as history has taken over, it secures and binds together, and does not allow them to slip away into the abyss of oblivion.

Now, I recognized this fact. I, Anna, the daughter of two royal personages, Alexius and Irene, born and bred in the purple. I was not ignorant of letters, for I carried my study of Greek to the highest pitch, and was also not unpractised in rhetoric; I perused the works of Aristotle and the dialogues of Plato carefully, and enriched my mind by the "quaternion" of learning. (I must let this out and it is not bragging to state what nature and my zeal for learning have given me, and the gifts which God apportioned to me at birth and time has contributed).

Alexius I

However, to resume—I intend in this writing of mine to recount the deeds done by my father so they should certainly not be lost in silence, or swept away, as it were, on the current of time into the sea of forgetfulness, and I shall recount not only his achievements as Emperor, but also the services he rendered to various Emperors before he himself received the sceptre.

These deeds I am going to relate, not in order to shew off my proficiency in letters, but that matters of such importance should not be left unattested for future generations. For even the greatest of deeds, if not haply preserved in written words and handed down to remembrance, become extinguished in the obscurity of silence.

---

[*] *A quotation from the Greek playwright Sophocles.*

Sermon to the Birds
Francis of Assisi (c. 1200)

This story comes from Little Flowers of St. Francis of Assisi. *Originally written in the early 1300s, nearly 100 years after of the death of Francis, it probably reflects a measure of idealism about his life. However, as this anecdote shows, Francis celebrated the beauty of nature and wanted all things to praise God. This translation by Roger Hudleston has been slightly updated.*

And as he went on his way, with great fervour, St. Francis lifted up his eyes, and saw on some trees by the wayside a great multitude of birds; and being much surprised, he said to his companions, "Wait for me here by the way, while I go and preach to my little sisters the birds."

And entering into the field, he began to preach to the birds which were on the ground, and suddenly all those also on the trees came round him, and all listened while St. Francis preached to them, and did not fly away until he had given them his blessing. And Brother Masseo related afterwards to Brother James of Massa how St. Francis went among them and even touched them with his garments, and how none of them moved. Now the substance of the sermon was this:

> *My little sisters the birds, you owe much to God, your Creator, and you ought to sing his praise at all times and in all places, because he has given you liberty to fly about into all places; and though you neither spin nor sew, he has given you a twofold and a threefold clothing for yourselves and for your offspring.*

> *Two of all your species he sent into the Ark with Noah that you might not be lost to the world; besides which, he feeds you, though you neither sow nor reap. He has given you fountains and rivers to quench your thirst, mountains and valleys in which to take refuge, and trees in which to build your nests; so that your Creator loves you much, having thus favoured you with such bounties. Beware, my little sisters, of the sin of ingratitude, and study always to give praise to God.*

As he said these words, all the birds began to open their beaks, to stretch their necks, to spread their wings and reverently to bow their heads to the ground, endeavouring by their motions and by their songs to manifest their joy to St. Francis. And the saint rejoiced with them. He wondered to see such a multitude of birds, and was charmed with their beautiful variety, with their attention and familiarity, for all which he devoutly gave thanks to the Creator.

Statue of Francis in Puerto Suarez, Bolivia

The Sarashina Diary
Takasué's Daughter (c. 1021)

The Mongols under Kublai Khan attempted and failed to conquer Japan in the 1270s and 1280s. This selection gives a look at life in Japan in the centuries before the Mongol invasions. The author of this diary was the daughter of a Japanese official, Fujiwara Takasué, but we do not know her name. She was born around 1008. In 1017 she moved with her father to another province of which he was appointed governor. They returned to the royal city of Kyoto in 1021, and that journey is where her diary begins. She continued to keep a diary until she was in her fifties.

I was brought up in a distant province which lies farther than the farthest end of the Eastern Road. I am ashamed to think that inhabitants of the Royal City will think me an uncultured girl.

Somehow I came to know that there are such things as romances in the world and wished to read them. When there was nothing to do by day or at night, one tale or another was told me by my elder sister or stepmother, and I heard several chapters about the shining Prince Genji. My longing for such stories increased, but how could they recite them all from memory? I became very

This illustration is from a later edition (c. 1100) of the book about Prince Genji that Takasué's daughter enjoyed.

restless and got an image of Yakushi Buddha made as large as myself. When I was alone I washed my hands and went secretly before the altar and prayed to him with all my life, bowing my head down to the floor. "Please let me go to the Royal City. There I can find many tales. Let me read all of them."

When thirteen years old, I was taken to the Royal City. On the third of the Long-moon month*, I went to Imataté, the old house where I had played as a child being broken up. At sunset in the foggy twilight, just as I was getting into the litter, I thought of the Buddha before which I had gone secretly to pray—I was sorry and secretly shed tears to leave him behind.

Outside of my new house there is no fence nor even shutters, but we have hung curtains and *sudaré***. From that house, standing on a low bluff, a wide plain extends towards the South. On the East and West the sea creeps close, so it is an interesting place. When fogs are falling it is so charming that I rise early every morning to see them. Sorry to leave this place.

On the fifteenth, in heavy dark rain, we crossed the boundary of the Province and lodged at Ikada in the Province of Shimofusa. Our lodging is almost submerged. I am so afraid I cannot sleep. I see only three lone trees standing on a little hill in the waste.

The next day was passed in drying our dripping clothes and waiting for the others to come up.

continued

---

* *September*
** *a bamboo privacy curtain*

On the seventeenth, started early in the morning, and crossed a deep river. I heard that in this Province there lived in olden times a chieftain of Mano. He had thousand and ten thousand webs of cloth woven and dipped them in the river* which now flows over the place where his great house stood. Four of the large gate-posts remained standing in the river.

Hearing the people composing poems about this place, I in my mind:

Had I not seen erect in the river
These solid timbers of the olden time
How could I know, how could I feel
The story of that house?

That evening we lodged at the beach of Kurodo. The white sand stretched far and wide. The pinewood was dark, the moon was bright, and the soft blowing of the wind made me lonely. People were pleased and composed poems. My poem:

For this night only
The autumn moon at Kurodo beach shall shine for me,
For this night only! — I cannot sleep.

Early in the morning we left this place and came to the Futoi River on the boundary between Shimofusa and Musashi. We lodged at the ferry of Matsusato near Kagami's rapids, and all night long our luggage was being carried over.

My nurse had lost her husband and gave birth to her child at the boundary of the Province, so we had to go up to the Royal City separately. I was longing for my nurse and wanted to go to see her, and was brought there by my elder brother in his arms. We, though in a temporary lodging, covered ourselves with warm cotton batting, but my nurse, as there was no man to take care of her, was lying in a wild place, covered only with coarse matting. She was in her red dress.

The moon came in, lighting up everything, and in the moonlight she looked transparent. I thought her very white and pure. She wept and caressed me, and I was loath to leave her. Even when I went with lingering heart, her image remained with me, and there was no interest in the changing scenes.

The next morning we crossed the river in a ferryboat in our litters. The persons who had come with us thus far in their own conveyances went back from this place. We, who were going up to the Royal City, stayed here for a while to follow them with our eyes; and as it was a parting for life all wept. Even my childish heart felt sorrow.

This Buddhist temple was built near Kyoto during the time this diary was written.

---

for bleaching

52

Mongol Customs of War
Marco Polo (c. 1300)

In The Travels of Marco Polo, *the author described the customs of the Mongols, who had recently taken control of China. This text is from the 1903 translation, annotated by Henry Yule and Henri Cordier. At the time of this translation, the word "Tartar" was generally used in Western Europe and America to describe the Mongolian people. In this excerpt, we have updated "Tartar" to "Mongol," the name more commonly used today.*

All their harness of war is excellent and costly. Their arms are bows and arrows, sword and mace; but above all the bow, for they are capital archers, indeed the best that are known. On their backs they wear armour of boiled leather, prepared from buffalo and other hides, which is very strong. They are excellent soldiers, and passing valiant in battle.

They are also more capable of hardships than other nations; for many a time, if need be, they will go for a month without any supply of food, living only on the milk of their mares and on such game as their bows may win them. Their horses also will subsist entirely on the grass of the plains, so that there is no need to carry store of barley or straw or oats; and they are very docile to their riders. These, in case of need, will abide on horseback the livelong night, armed at all points, while the horse will be continually grazing.

Of all troops in the world these are they which endure the greatest hardship and fatigue, and which cost the least; and they are the best of all for making wide conquests of country. And this you will perceive from what you have heard and shall hear in this book; and (as a fact) there can be no manner of doubt that now they are the masters of the biggest half of the world. Their troops are admirably ordered in the manner that I shall now relate.

You see, when a Mongol prince goes forth to war, he takes with him, say, 100,000 horse. Well, he appoints an officer to every ten men, one to every hundred, one to every thousand, and one to every ten thousand, so that his own orders have to be given to ten persons only, and each of these ten persons has to pass the orders only to other ten, and so on; no one having to give orders to more than ten. And every one in turn is responsible only to the officer immediately over him; and the discipline and order that comes of this method is marvellous, for they are a people very obedient to their chiefs. . . .

And when the army is on the march they have always 200 horsemen, very well mounted, who are sent a distance of two marches in advance to reconnoitre, and these always keep ahead. They have a similar party detached in the rear, and on either flank, so that there is a good look-out kept on all sides against a surprise. When they are going on a distant expedition they take no gear with them except two leather bottles for milk; a little earthenware pot to cook their meat in, and a little tent to shelter them from rain. . . .

They also have milk dried into a kind of paste to carry with them; and when they need food they put this in water, and beat it up till it dissolves, and then drink it. It is prepared in this way; they boil the milk, and when the rich part floats on the top they skim it into another vessel, and of that they make butter; for the milk will not become solid till this is removed. Then they put the milk in the sun to dry.

And when they go on an expedition, every man takes some ten pounds of this dried milk with him. And of a morning he will take a half pound of it and put it in his leather bottle, with as much water as he pleases. So, as he rides along, the milk-paste and the water in the bottle get well churned together into a kind of pap, and that makes his dinner.

When they come to an engagement with the enemy, they will gain the victory in this fashion. They never let themselves get into a regular medley, but keep perpetually riding round and shooting into the enemy. And as they do not count it any shame to run away in battle, they will sometimes pretend to do so, and in running away they turn in the saddle and shoot hard and strong at the foe, and in this way make great havoc.

Mongol Warriors, Early 1300s

Their horses are trained so perfectly that they will double hither and thither, just like a dog, in a way that is quite astonishing. Thus they fight to as good purpose in running away as if they stood and faced the enemy, because of the vast volleys of arrows that they shoot in this way, turning round upon their pursuers, who are fancying that they have won the battle.

But when the Mongols see that they have killed and wounded a good many horses and men, they wheel round bodily, and return to the charge in perfect order and with loud cries; and in a very short time the enemy are routed. In truth they are stout and valiant soldiers, and inured to war. And you perceive that it is just when the enemy sees them run, and imagines that he has gained the battle, that he has in reality lost it; for the Mongols wheel round in a moment when they judge the right time has come. And after this fashion they have won many a fight.

All this that I have been telling you is true of the manners and customs of the genuine Mongols. But I must add also that in these days they are greatly degenerated; for those who are settled in Cathay have taken up the practices of the Idolaters of the country, and have abandoned their own institutions; while those who have settled in the Levant have adopted the customs of the Saracens.

The Rihla
Ibn Battuta (c. 1355)

Ibn Battuta was born in Tangier (now in Morocco, Africa) in 1304. He spent about 30 years of his life traveling throughout the Muslim world in Africa, southern Europe, the Middle East, and Asia. The following excerpt comes from his account of his travels, as translated by Samuel Lee (1783-1852), a British scholar.

India has long been an important part of world trade. Malabar refers to the area on the southwestern tip of the Indian peninsula.

In the country of Malabar are twelve kings, the greatest of whom has fifty thousand troops at his command; the least, five thousand or thereabouts. . . . Their country is that from which black pepper is brought; and this is the far greater part of their produce and culture.

The pepper tree resembles that of the dark grape. They plant it near that of the cocoa-nut, and make frame-work for it, just as they do for the grape tree. It has, however, no tendrils, and the tree itself resembles a bunch of grapes. The leaves are like the ears of a horse; but some of them resemble the leaves of a bramble. When the autumn arrives, it is ripe; they then cut it, and spread it just as they do grapes, and thus it is dried by the sun. As to what some have said, that they boil it in order to dry it, it is without foundation.

I also saw, in their country and on the sea-shores, aloes like the seed-aloe, sold by measure, just as meal and millet is. . . .

We next came to Calicut, one of the great ports of the district of Malabar, and in which merchants from all parts are found. The king of this place is an infidel, who shaves his chin just as the Haidari Fakeers of Room do.* When we approached this place, the people came out to meet us, and with a large concourse brought us into the port. The greatest part of the Muslim merchants of this place are so wealthy, that one of them can purchase the whole freightage of such vessels as put in here; and fit out others like them.

Here we waited three months for the season to set sail for China: for there is only one season in the year in which the sea of China is navigable. Nor then is the voyage undertaken, except in vessels of the three descriptions following: the greatest is called a junk, the middling sized a zaw, the least a kakam. The sails of these vessels are made of cane-reeds, woven together like a mat; which, when they put into port, they leave standing in the wind. In some of these vessels there will be employed a thousand men, six hundred of these sailors, and four hundred soldiers. Each of the larger ships is followed by three others, a middle-sized, a third-, and a fourth-sized.

These vessels are nowhere made except in the city of El Zaitun in China, or in Sin Kilan, which is Sin El Sin. They row in these ships with large oars, which may be compared to great masts, over some of which five and twenty men will be stationed, who work standing. The

---

* *Fakeers (or faqirs) were traveling Muslim teachers. "Room" (or Rome, meaning the Eastern Roman Empire) refers to the Byzantine Empire based in Constantinople.*

commander of each vessel is a great Emir. In the large ships too they sow garden herbs and ginger, which they cultivate in cisterns (made for that purpose and) placed on the sides of them. In these also are houses constructed of wood, in which the higher officers reside with their wives: but these they do not hire out to the merchants. Every vessel, therefore, is like an independent city. Of such ships as these, Chinese individuals will sometimes have large numbers: and, generally, the Chinese are the richest people in the world.

The Ibn Battuta Mall opened in 2005 in the United Arab Emirates. It has six courts that represent different areas visited by Ibn Battuta—Andalusia, Tunisia, Egypt, Persia, India, and China. The mall features this model of a Chinese ship like that described by Ibn Battuta.

Ibn Battuta also visited Constantinople, the capital of the Eastern Roman Empire. He said that he was accompanying the daughter of the Emperor of Constantinople.

We entered Constantinople about sun-set; they were then ringing their bells at such a rate, that the very horizon shook with the noise. When we came to the gate of the Emperor, the porters refused to admit us without a permission from the Emperor. Some of her followers, therefore, went and told them our case, and she requested permission of her father, stating our circumstances to him.

We were then allowed to enter, and were lodged in a house adjoining that of our lady, who sent our provisions morning and evening. The King also granted us a letter of safe conduct, permitting us to pass wherever we pleased about the city.

On the fourth day after our arrival, I was introduced to the Sultan Takfur, son of George, king of Constantinople. His father George was still living, but had retired from the world, become a monk, and given up the kingdom to his son.[*]

When I arrived at the fifth gate of the palace, which was guarded by soldiers, I was searched, lest I should carry any weapon with me; which is submitted to by every citizen, as well as stranger, who wishes to be introduced to the King. The same is observed by the Emperors of India.

I was introduced, therefore, and did homage. The Emperor was sitting upon his throne with his Queen, and daughter, our mistress; her brothers were seated beneath the throne. I was kindly received, and asked, as to my circumstances and arrival; also about Jerusalem, the Temple of the Resurrection, the Cradle of Jesus, Bethlehem, and the city of Abraham (or Hebron), then of Damascus, Egypt, Iraq, and the country of Room; to all of which I gave suitable replies.

A Jew was our interpreter. The King was much surprised at my tale; and said to his sons: "Let this man be treated honorably, and give him a letter of safe conduct." He then put a dress of honor on me, and ordered a saddled horse to be given me, with one of his own umbrellas, which with them is a mark of protection.

I then requested that he would appoint some one to ride about with me into the different quarters of the city, that I might see them. He made the appointment accordingly, and I rode about with the officer for some days, witnessing the wonders of the place.

Its largest church is that of Saint Sophia. I saw its outside only. Its interior I could not, because, just within the door there was a cross which every one who entered worshipped. It is said, that this church is one of the foundations of Asaf, the son of Barachias, and nephew of Solomon. The churches, monasteries, and other places of worship within the city, are almost innumerable.

---

[*] *Ibn Battuta is evidently referring to Andronikos II, who had abdicated the throne in 1328 when he was ousted by his grandson, who became Andronikos III.*

The Song of Joan of Arc
Christine de Pisan (1429)

Christine de Pisan was born in 1364, and her father saw that she received a strong education. After she was widowed in 1387, she became a professional writer to support herself and her young children. Christine became the official court historian of France—the first woman to hold that position. She wrote historical works, instructional material, and poetry. She advanced the idea that men and women had equal value and ability. The image at left depicts Christine giving a book to the Queen of France.

Christine retired to a convent in 1418, but she wrote one final poem in 1429 to honor Joan of Arc. Christine died the next year. "The Song of Joan of Arc" is a lengthy poem, but here is short excerpt. "The Maid" refers to Joan.

The translation is by Ben D. Kennedy (www.maidofheaven.com).

And you Charles, now King of France
the seventh in your noble line
You suffered such misfortune and
disgrace before receiving aid divine.
Thanks to God your honor is renewed
by the Maid who has laid low your
enemies beneath your standard of blue.
And this is something very new!

In such a short time, when all thought
that it was quite impossible for you to
recover your country even if you fought,
Once it was lost but now it is yours
despite all those who harmed your heart,
you have recovered it. And all due to
the intelligence of the Maid who, thanks
to God, most expertly played her part.

A painting of Joan of Arc was made during her life, but it has not survived. This artist's depiction of Joan is from about 1485.

Letter to the Aldermen of Culm
The Schoeffen of Magdeburg (1338)

The German city of Magdeburg was a prominent trading center before the establishment of the Hanseatic League. This letter sheds light on legal practices in the 1300s as the Schoeffen of Magdeburg answer questions from the aldermen of another town called Culm (now known as Chelmno, Poland). "Schoeffen" refers to the leading men of a town, something like a town council. The "Burggrave" was the noble in charge of a certain area, and the "burgomaster" and "schultheiss" were like city mayors. This text is from A Source Book for Medieval History *(1905), edited by Oliver Thatcher and Edgar McNeal.*

1. May aldermen be deposed? To the honorable aldermen of Culm, we the Schoeffen of Magdeburg, your obedient servants [send greetings]. You have asked us in your letter whether aldermen may choose other aldermen, and whether they may choose from among themselves burgomasters and Schoeffen without the consent of the burggrave. And also whether the burggrave may depose some of the aldermen and appoint others in their place. We answer, that the aldermen may choose other aldermen for a year, and one or two burgomasters from their own number also for a year. But the burggrave has no right to depose aldermen and put others in their place.

2. Who shall choose other Schoeffen? The Schoeffen shall elect other Schoeffen, and those elected shall remain Schoeffen as long as they live. The aldermen have no right to elect Schoeffen. The burggrave shall confirm the Schoeffen who are elected.

3. May the aldermen make laws? You have also asked us whether the aldermen with the consent of their citizens may make laws among themselves and fix the penalties for offenses against them, without the consent of the burggrave, and whether the aldermen have the right to collect such penalties and retain them, or shall the burggrave and the Schultheiss have a share in them. And you have also asked if a man breaks the laws and refuses to pay the fine, how it is to be collected from him.

continued

The town of Magdeburg is located on the Elbe River. Construction of Magdeburg Cathedral, shown on the left, began in 1209. The steeples were finally completed in 1520.

We answer, that the aldermen may make laws and fix their penalties provided these laws do not conflict with the laws of the city. And they may do this without the consent of the burggrave. And they have the right to demand the payment of fines, and they may keep them for the benefit of the city; the burggrave and the Schultheiss shall have no part in them.

4. What if a man refuses to pay a fine? If a man refuses to pay a fine but admits that he owes it, the aldermen may seize and imprison him until he pays it. If he says he does not owe the fine, he shall prove it by taking an oath by the saints.

5. About false measures. You have further asked whether the aldermen have jurisdiction over weights and measures, false measures, and the sale of provisions, and if a man refuses to pay a fine how it shall be collected. We answer, that aldermen have jurisdiction over the said things, and that if a man refuses to pay his fine, they may seize and imprison him until he pays it as written above.

6. About damage done to a forest. You asked us if a man cuts wood in a forest, how he shall pay the damage. We answer, if a man cuts down trees in another's forest, or cuts his grass, or fishes in his streams, he shall pay for the damage and fine besides.

7. How far shall a guest live from the city? You also asked us how far a man must live from court if he wishes to have the right of a guest. We answer, if a guest is accused before the court, if he swears by the saints that he lives more than twelve miles from the court, he shall have his trial at once. If a guest enters suit against a citizen in the same court, the citizen shall answer in court that same day if the guest demands it.

8. About attaching the property of a guest.* You further asked us how you should proceed, if a man attaches the property of a guest from a far country, so that justice may be done to both. We answer, if a man attaches the property of a guest who lives so far away that you cannot get hold of him, the attachment is not to be put into execution until the guest is informed of it. If the guest does not then appear to defend his property, the attached property may be taken.

9. About taxes. You further asked us, if the citizens have property outside of the territory of the city which they hold from some lord and from which they receive an income, are they bound to pay the tax which may be assessed on property outside the city, just the same as they do on their ordinary property? We answer, that according to the law and practice of our city, every man must pay taxes on his property outside as well as inside the city, no matter where it is, and he must take an oath to its value and pay a tax accordingly.

The Church of St. James and St. Nicholas in Chelmno, Poland, was originally completed in the 1300s and rebuilt in the 1800s.

If one person fails to pay a debt he owes to another person, a court may decide that the debtor's property should be taken or sold to repay the debt. This is called "attaching property."

John 1:1-9
Wycliffe Translation (c. 1390)

This portion of Scripture is translated in the English of the late 1300s. English spelling and pronunciation were different from what they are today, so reading this can be hard. Read the words out loud to help you understand what they mean. If you have trouble, compare this translation with the Bible you usually read.

1. In the bigynnyng was the word, and the word was at God, and God was the word.
2. This was in the bigynnyng at God.
3. Alle thingis weren maad bi hym, and withouten hym was maad no thing, that thing that was maad.
4. In hym was liif, and the liif was the liyt of men; and the liyt schyneth in derknessis,
5. and derknessis comprehendiden not it.
6. A man was sent fro God, to whom the name was Joon.
7. This man cam in to witnessyng, that he schulde bere witnessing of the liyt, that alle men schulden bileue bi hym.
8. He was not the liyt, but that he schulde bere witnessing of the liyt.
9. There was a very liyt, which liytneth ech man that cometh in to this world.

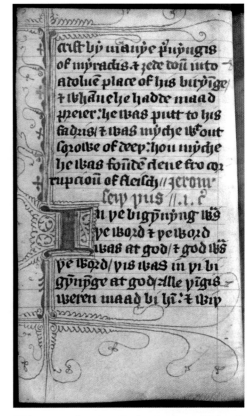

This page, showing the beginning of John 1, is from a 14th-century copy of the Wycliffe translation of the New Testament. It is a pocket-sized manuscript that could have been carried by a traveling preacher.

Architecture in Asia and Africa

Zheng He's expeditions visited numerous parts of Asia and Africa. These photos show local architecture that existed in these regions at the time the Chinese visited. Modern country names are given in parentheses.

The My Son area (Vietnam) contains numerous Hindu temples built by the Champa people over several centuries up to the 1200s.

The Brihadisvara is a Hindu temple built in the early 1000s by the Chola Dynasty (southern India).

The Muarajambi Temple Compound is a collection of Buddhist temples on the island of Sumatra (Indonesia). This is one of many structures built there between the 600s and 1300s.

The Fakhr Ad-Din Mosque in Mogadishu (Somalia) was completed in 1269.

Great Zimbabwe

Spread across southern Africa are about 200 sites with the remains of large stone walls and towers built without mortar. The largest of these sites, called Great Zimbabwe, was built by the Shona people between about 1100 and 1450. Archaeologists have discovered glass beads and porcelain from Persia and China and Arab coins from East Africa. These photographs show different views of the complex.

Vicente Pegado, a Portuguese captain, visited and described Great Zimbabwe in 1531. Other Europeans visited in the 19th century.

The modern country of Zimbabwe, established in 1980, took its name from this ancient monument. The Zimbabwe Bird, used on the national flag and currency, is based on bird statues found at the Great Zimbabwe site.

Fall of Constantinople

The news that Constantinople had fallen took one month to reach the island of Crete, which was at the time a colony of Venice. This short note was found on a Greek manuscript that is now held by the British Museum. This translation by W. L. North is used with his permission.

In the year 1453, on June 29, a Friday, there came from Constantinople three Cretan caravels—those of Sgouros, Hyalina, and Philomatos. They said that on the 29th of May, the third day of Saint Theodosia, at the third hour of the morning[*], the Hagarenes, that is the troops of Mehmet Celebi, entered the city of Constantinople. They also said that they killed the emperor, the Lord Constantine Dragas and Palaiologos. Then there was great sorrow and much weeping on Crete because of the sad news that had arrived. Indeed nothing worse than this has ever happened or ever will happen. May the Lord God be merciful to us and free us from His fearful threats.

Venetian Fort Built on Crete in the 1370s

---

[*] *9:00 am*

International Trade and Coins

Venice was a leader in international trade for many centuries. The illustrations on this page highlight the types of items traded during the 15th century.

This copper ewer from Venice has enamel and gold decorations (c. 1500).

This Venetian textile is made of silk velvet and has a pomegranate pattern (c. 1480).

Spices from India were in high demand in other parts of the world. This photograph shows spices at a modern market in Goa, India.

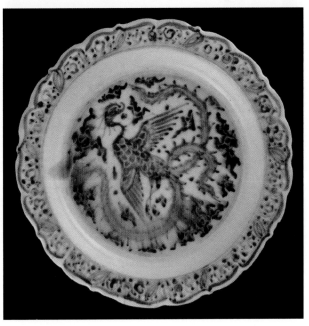

This ceramic bowl from Syria reflects the influence of Chinese designs (1400s).

Clockwise from top left, these gold coins are from Egypt, Hungary, Holland, and Iraq

Royal Commentaries of the Inca
Garcilaso de la Vega (1609)

Garcilaso de la Vega (1539-1616) was the son of an Inca noblewoman and a Spanish conquistador. As he grew up, he learned from his mother and others in his community about the history of the Inca people. After he moved to Spain in 1560, he compiled this history into Royal Commentaries of the Incas. *His book was first published in Spanish in 1609. This excerpt is from the English translation by Paul Rycaut, printed in 1688. Some of the text has been modernized.*

They had attained so much Geometry as served them for to measure out their Lands, and make out limits and bounds to their several partitions; but this was not done in an artificial manner, but by their lines, and small stones, which they used in all their Accounts.

As to their Geography, they knew how to decypher in colours the Model of every Nation, with the distinct Provinces, and how they were bounded. I have seen an exact Map of Cuzco, with the parts adjacent, and the four principal ways to it, perfectly described in a sort of Mortar, compounded with small stones and straw, which delineated all the places, both great and small, with the broad Streets, and narrow Lanes, and Houses which were ancient and decayed, and with the three streams running through it, all which were described with great curiosity.

Moreover in this Draught the Hills and Valleys, the turnings and windings of the Rivers were made to appear so plain, that the best Cosmographer in the World could not have exceeded it. The use of this Model was to inform the Visitors, which they called *Damian*, of the extent and division of the Countries, whensoever they went by the King's Commission to survey the Province, and number the people within the precincts of Cuzco, and other places; this Model which I mention, was made in Muyna, which the Spaniards call now Mohina, and is distant about five Leagues from the City of Cuzco towards the Zur; the which I had opportunity to observe, being then present with the Visitors, who went to number the Indians that inhabited the Division of Garcilaso de la Vega, My Lord and Master.

In Arithmetick they knew much, and were skilled in a peculiar manner and nature in that Science; for by certain knots of divers colours they summed up all the accounts of Tribute, and Contributions, belonging to the revenue of the Inca; and thereby knew how to account, and discount, to subtract, and to multiply; but to proportion the respective Taxes on every Nation by way of division, they performed it in another

Garcilaso de la Vega

manner by grains of Maize, or Pebbles, which served in the place of Counters. And because it was necessary that Accounts should be kept of all charges relating to War and Peace, that the People, and the Flocks and Herds of Cattle should be numbered, that the payment of Tributes, and the like, should be registered and noted, there were certain Persons appointed for that work, who made it their study and business to be ready and skilfull in Accounts; and because perhaps one Person was appointed to keep the reckonings of three or four distinct things, as Accountant General, which seems difficult to be performed by the way of their threads and knots, we shall discourse it hereafter more at large, in what manner they distinguished their Accounts of divers businesses.

In Musick they arrived to a Certain Harmony, in which the Indians of Colla did more particularly excell, having been the Inventors of a certain Pipe made of Canes glued together, every one of which having a different Note of higher and lower, in the manner of Organs, made a pleasing Musick by the dissonancy of sounds, the Treble, Tenor and Basse, exactly corresponding and answering each to other; with these Pipes they often played in concert, and made tolerable Musick, though they wanted the Quavers, Semiquavers, Aires, and many Voices which perfect the Harmony amongst us. They had also other Pipes, which were Flutes with four or five stops, like the Pipes of Shepherds; with these they played not in concert, but singly, and tuned them to Sonnets, which they composed in metre, the Subject of which was love, and the Passions which arise from the Favours or Displeasures of a Mistress. These Musicians were Indians trained up in that art for divertisement of the Incas, and the Curacas, who were his Nobles, which, as rustical and barbarous as it was, it was not common, but acquired with great Industry and Study.

Every Song was set to its proper Tune; for two Songs of different Subjects could not correspond with the same Aire, by reason that the Musick which the Gallant made on his Flute, was designed to express the satisfaction or discontent of his Mind, which were not so intelligible perhaps by the words as by the melancholy or cheerfulness of the Tune which he played.

The Songs which they composed of their Wars, and grand Achievements, were never set to the Aires of their Flute, being too grave and serious to be intermixed with the pleasures and softnesses of Love; for these were only sung at their principal Festivals when they commemorated their Victories and Triumphs.

Garcilaso de la Vega was born in what became the modern country of Peru. He has been remembered in Peru with a university and a football (soccer) stadium named after him.

Chinese Poetry from the Ming Dynasty
(1300s-1400s)

Liu Ji (also known as Bowen) lived from 1311-1375. He was an adviser to Zhu Yuanzhang, who founded the Ming Dynasty. Chao Ts'ai-chi was a female poet in the 1400s. These translations are from Chinese Poetry in English Verse *(1898) by Herbert A. Giles.*

I mounted when the cock had just begun,
And reached the convent ere the bells were done.
A gentle zephyr whispered o'er the lawn;
Behind the wood the moon gave way to dawn.

And in this pure sweet solitude I lay,
Stretching my limbs out to await the day.
No sound along the willow pathway dim
Save the soft echo of the bonzes' hymn.

Liu Ji

A centenarian 'mongst men
Is rare; and if one comes, what then?
The mightiest heroes of the past
Upon the hillside sleep at last.

Liu Ji

The tide in the river beginning to rise,
Near the sad hour of parting, brings tears to our eyes;
Alas that these furlongs of willow-strings gay
Cannot hold fast the boat that will soon be away!

Chao Ts'ai-chi

Letter from Michelangelo to His Father
(1497)

Michelangelo went to Rome in 1496 at the age of 21. The next year he wrote this letter to his father. It is taken from Robert W. Carden's book Michelangelo: A Record of His Life as Told in His Own Letters and Papers *(1913).*

Domino Lodovico Buonarroti,
      in Florence.

In the name of God, this First day of July, 1497.

Most Revered and Dear Father, — You must not be surprised that I have not yet returned to you, for I have failed in all my attempts to settle my business with the Cardinal, and I have no wish to leave Rome until I have received satisfaction and have been paid for my work. With these exalted personages one has to go slowly, for they cannot be forced into action. I believe, however, that the end of the coming week will certainly see all my affairs arranged.

I must tell you that Fra Lionardo has returned here to Rome, and says he was obliged to flee from Viterbo and that his frock has been taken away from him. He wished to return to you: wherefore I gave him a gold ducat for his journey, which he asked of me. I think you must already know of this, for by now he ought to be with you.

I know of nothing else I have to tell you, for I am surrounded by uncertainties and know not as yet which way matters will turn: but I hope soon to be with you once more. I am well, and trust that you are the same. Commend me to my friends.

Michelagniolo,
Sculptor, in Rome.

Later in 1497, Michelangelo received the commission to create his famous Pietà. *He completed that statue in 1499 at the age of 24.*

The Destruction of the Indies
Bartolomé de las Casas (1552)

Bartolomé de las Casas (1484-1566) was a Spanish priest who became horrified at the way his fellow Spanish, "who pride themselves in the Name of Christians," treated the natives in the West Indies and the Americas. He attempted to raise awareness of the problem with Spanish authorities and was named the first Protector of Indians in the Spanish colonies. He published A Short Account of the Destruction of the Indies *in 1552. This excerpt is from a 1689 English edition.*

America was discovered and found out Ann. Dom.* 1492, and the Year insuing inhabited by the Spaniards, and afterward a multitude of them travelled thither from Spain for the space of Nine and Forty Years. . . .

As to the firm land, we are certainly satisfied, and assur'd, that the Spaniards by their barbarous and execrable Actions have absolutely depopulated Ten Kingdoms, of greater extent than all Spain, together with the Kingdoms of Arragon and Portugal, that is to say, above One Thousand Miles, which now lie waste and desolate, and are absolutely ruined, when as formerly no other Country whatsoever was more populous. Nay we dare boldly affirm, that during the Forty Years space, wherein they exercised their sanguinary and detestable Tyranny in these Regions, above Twelve Millions (computing Men, Women, and Children) have undeservedly perished; nor do I conceive that I should deviate from the Truth by saying that above Fifteen Millions in all paid their last Debt to Nature. . . .

Now the ultimate end and scope that incited the Spaniards to endeavor the Extirpation and Desolation of this People, was Gold only; that thereby growing opulent in a short time, they might arrive at once at such Degrees and Dignities, as were no wayes consistent with their Persons.

Bartolomé de las Casas

---

* *Abbreviation for* Anno Domini, *Year of Our Lord* (AD)

Letter to the King and Queen of Castille
King Manuel (1499)

King Manuel of Portugal sent a letter to Ferdinand and Isabella of Castille to announce the successful voyage of Vasco da Gama (Manuel was their son-in-law). This excerpt is from A Journal of the First Voyage of Vasco Da Gama, 1497-1499, *translated and edited by E. G. Ravenstein.*

Your Highnesses already know that we had ordered Vasco da Gama, a nobleman of our household, and his brother Paulo da Gama, with four vessels to make discoveries by sea, and that two years have now elapsed since their departure. And as the principal motive of this enterprise has been, with our predecessors, the service of God our Lord, and our own advantage, it pleased Him in His mercy to speed them on their route.

From a message which has now been brought to this city by one of the captains, we learn that they did reach and discover India and other kingdoms and lordships bordering upon it; that they entered and navigated its sea, finding large cities, large edifices and rivers, and great populations, among whom is carried on all the trade in spices and precious stones, which are forwarded in ships (which these same explorers saw and met with in good numbers and of great size) to Mecca, and thence to Cairo, whence they are dispersed throughout the world.

Manuel

Of these they have brought a quantity, including cinnamon, cloves, ginger, nutmeg, and pepper, as well as other kinds, together with the boughs and leaves of the same; also many fine stones of all sorts, such as rubies and others. And they also came to a country in which there are mines of gold, of which, as of the spices and precious stones, they did not bring as much as they could have done, for they took no merchandise with them.

Letter to Katherine Luther
Martin Luther (1546)

Martin Luther, a former monk, and Katharine von Bora, a former nun, were married in 1525. They reared six children of their own along with seven children of relatives. The Luthers enjoyed a form of bowling in their yard, played chess, and made music together. Martin and Katherine Luther exchanged many letters during their marriage.

Near the end of his life, Luther traveled to his hometown of Eisleben to help two brothers settle a personal dispute. This letter was written to Katherine one week before Martin suffered a stroke and died. This translation is from The Letters of Martin Luther, *translated by Margaret A. Currie (1908). Katherine, pictured below, died six years later.*

February 10, 1546

To the saintly, anxious lady, Katherine Luther, owner of Zulsdorf, at Wittenberg, my gracious dear wife. Grace and peace in Christ!

Most saintly lady doctoress, we thank you kindly for your great care for us, which prevented you sleeping, for since you began to be so anxious we were nearly consumed by a fire in our inn just outside my room door; and yesterday, doubtless on account of your anxiety, a stone fell upon our heads and almost crushed us as in a mouse-trap; and over and above, in our own private room, lime and mortar came down for two days, and when the masons came—after only touching the stone with two fingers—it fell, and was as large as a large pillow, and two hand-breadths wide.

Katherine Luther

We had to thank your anxious care for all this, but happily the dear, holy angels guarded us also. I fear if you do not cease being anxious, the earth may at last swallow us up and the elements pursue us. Is it thus thou hast learnt the catechism and the Faith? Pray and leave it to God to care for us, as He has promised in the 55th Psalm and many other places, "Cast thy burden on the Lord, and He shall sustain thee."

Thank God we are fresh and well, except that we are getting tired of the whole business, and nothing would satisfy Dr. Jonas but to have a sore leg also, having knocked it against a chest; so great is the power of human envy, that he would not permit me to be the sole possessor of a lame leg. I herewith commit you to God. We would gladly be free and set out on our homeward journey, if God permitted it.

Amen. Amen. Amen. Your obedient servant,

Martin Luther

Advice to a Servant

Roger Ascham (1559)

Roger Ascham (c. 1515-1568) was an English scholar. He tutored young Princess Elizabeth, later Queen, in Greek and Latin. He wrote a letter to his brother-in-law when the latter became a servant to the Earl of Warwick. This excerpt was included in an 1868 publication called Early English Meals and Manners. *The spelling and punctuation have been slightly updated for clarity.*

First and formost, in all your thoughts, words, and deeds, have before your eyes the fear of God. . . . Love and serve your lord* willingly, faithfully, and secretly. Love and live with your fellows honestly, quietly, and courteously, that no man have cause either to hate you for your stubborn frowardness,** or to malice you for your proud ungentleness, two faults which commonly young men soonest fall into in great men's service.

Contemn*** no poor man, mock no simple man, which proud fools in court like and love to do. Find fault with your self and with none other, the best way to live honestly and quietly in the court. Carry no tales, be no common teller of news. Be not inquisitive of other men's talk, for those that are desirous to hear what they need not, commonly be ready to babble what they should not.

Use not to lye, for that is unhonest; speak not every truth, for that is unneedfull . . . Use not diceing nor carding.**** The more you use them the less you will be esteemed; the cunninger you be at them the worse man you will be counted.

For pastime, love and learn that which your lord liketh and useth most, whether it be riding, shooting, hunting, hawking, fishing or any such exercise. Beware of secret corners and night sitting up, the two nurses of mischief, unthriftiness, loss, and sickness. Beware chiefly of idleness, the great pathway that leadeth directly to all evils.

Be diligent always, be present every where in your lord's service, be at hand to call others, and be not often sent for yourself. For mark this as part of your creed, that the good service of one whole year shall never get so much as the absence of one hour may lose, when your lord shall stand in need of you to send. If you consider always that absence and negligence must needs be cause of grief and sorrow to your self, of chiding and rueing to your lord, and that duty done diligently and presently shall gain you profit, and purchase you great praise and your lord's good countenance, you shall rid me of care, and win your self credit, make me a glad man, and your aged mother a joyful woman, and breed your friends great comfort. Soe I commit and commend you to God's merciful protection and good guidance, who long preserve Your ever loving and affectionate brother in law.

---

* *referring to the servant's employer*
** *being contrary, not easily managed*
*** *look down on, regard with contempt*
**** *Don't play dice or card games.*

74

Speech to the Troops at Tilbury
Elizabeth I (1588)

As the Spanish prepared to invade England, Queen Elizabeth I visited the English army camped at Tilbury. The speech she made to encourage them has been recorded in different forms by different authors. The following version is from a letter written many years later by Leonel Sharp, who had been a chaplain at the time of the Spanish Armada. Historians generally agree that it matches Elizabeth's style. The painting by Robert Peake the Elder shows Elizabeth being carried by her courtiers (c. 1600).

The Queen the next morning rode through all the Squadrons of her Army, as Armed Pallas, attended by Noble Footmen, Leicester, Essex, and Norris, then Lord Marshal, and divers other great Lords. Where she made an excellent Oration to her Army, which the next day after her departure, I was commanded to re-deliver to all the Army together, to keep a Publick Fast.

Her words were these:

> My loving people, we have been persuaded by some that are careful of our safety, to take heed how we commit our self to armed multitudes, for fear of treachery: but I assure you, I do not desire to live to distrust my faithful and loving people. Let Tyrants fear, I have alwayes so behaved my self, that under God I have placed my chiefest strength and safeguard in the loyal hearts and good will of my subjects.

> And therefore I am come amongst you, as you see, at this time, not for my recreation, and disport, but being resolved, in the midst and heat of the battle, to live or die amongst you all, to lay down for my God, and for my Kingdom, and for my people, my Honour, and my blood, even in the dust.

> I know I have the body but of a weak and feeble woman, but I have the heart and Stomach of a King, and of a King of England too, and think foul scorn that Parma or Spain, or any Prince of Europe, should dare to invade the borders of my Realm; to which rather then any dishonour shall grow by me, I my self will take up arms, I my self will be your General, Judge, and Rewarder of every one of your virtues in the field.

> I know already for your forwardness, you have deserved rewards, and crowns and we do assure you, in the word of a Prince, they shall be duly paid you. In the mean time, my Lieutenant General shall be in my stead, then whom never Prince commanded a more Noble or worthy subject, not doubting but by your obedience to my General, by your Concord in the Camp, and your valour in the field, we shall shortly have a famous victory over those enemies of my God, of my Kingdoms, and of my People.

Jewish Synagogue and Cemetery

One of the most influential students from the Jewish university at Lublin was Moses Isserles, known as Rema (or Remuh). Rema returned to his hometown of Krakow, Poland, to establish another yeshiva. He also served as rabbi of a synagogue established in Krakow in the 1550s. Rema studied history, astronomy, and philosophy, but he is especially remembered for his commentary on and application of Jewish law.

The current synagogue in Krakow has elements that date back to 1557, but it has undergone extensive renovation. Exterior and interior views are shown at left. Rema, who died in 1572, is buried in the cemetery beside the synagogue. His tombstone is shown at right.

The True History of the Conquest of New Spain
Bernal Diaz del Castillo (1568)

Bernal Diaz del Castillo (c. 1495-1584) was a Spanish soldier under Hernando Cortés during the conquest of Mexico. Diaz settled in New Spain, became a public official, and wrote his memoirs, The True History of the Conquest of New Spain. *This excerpt is from an 1844 translation by John Ingram Lockhart. It describes the Spanish soldiers visiting the Great Temple in Tenochtitlan, the Aztec capital, in 1519. The Spanish climbed 114 steps to the top of the temple and met with the Aztec ruler Montezuma.*

"Ascending this temple, Malinche," said [Montezuma] to our commander, "must certainly have fatigued you!" Cortés, however, assured him, through our interpreters, that it was not possible for anything to tire us. Upon this the monarch took hold of his hand and invited him to look down and view his vast metropolis, with the towns which were built in the lake, and the other towns which surrounded the city. Montezuma also observed, that from this place we should have a better view of the great market.

Indeed, this infernal temple, from its great height, commanded a view of the whole surrounding neighbourhood. From this place we could likewise see the three causeways which led into Mexico,—that from Iztapalapan, by which we had entered the city four days ago; that from Tlacupa, along which we took our flight eight months after, when we were beaten out of the city by the new monarch Cuitlahuatzin; the third was that of Tepeaquilla. We also observed the aqueduct which ran from Chapultepec, and provided the whole town with sweet water. We could also distinctly see the bridges across the openings, by which these causeways were intersected, and through which the waters of the lake ebbed and flowed. The lake itself was crowded with canoes, which were bringing provisions, manufactures, and other merchandise to the city. From here we also discovered that the only communication of the houses in this city, and of all the other towns built in the lake, was by means of drawbridges or canoes. In all these towns the beautiful white plastered temples rose above the smaller ones, like so many towers and castles in our Spanish towns, and this, it may be imagined, was a splendid sight.

After we had sufficiently gazed upon this magnificent picture, we again turned our eyes toward the great market, and beheld the vast numbers of buyers and sellers who thronged there. The bustle and noise occasioned by this multitude of human beings was so great that it could be heard at a distance of more than four miles. Some of our men, who had been at Constantinople and Rome, and travelled through the whole of Italy, said that they never had seen a market-place of such large dimensions, or which was so well regulated, or so crowded with people as this one at Mexico.

The Spanish destroyed the temple in 1521. The temple ruins were discovered in Mexico City in the 1900s. This model, located at the National Museum of Anthropology there, illustrates how the temple complex may have looked.

A Visit to the Wife of Suleyman
(c. 1550)

A girl known as Roxelana was born around 1504 in the town of Rohatyn, now in the country of Ukraine. She was captured and sold as a slave to the Turks. Suleyman took her as a concubine and later broke with Ottoman tradition by officially marrying her. She became known as Hürrem Sultan.

An unknown visitor from Genoa, perhaps the wife of a merchant, wrote a letter about her visit to Hürrem's residence. The translation on the next page is taken from The World's Story: A History of the World in Story, Song, and Art: Volume VI *(1914), edited by Eva March Tappan.*

The photo below shows a monument to Roxelana in Rohatyn.

When I entered the kiosk in which she lives, I was received by many eunuchs in splendid costume blazing with jewels, and carrying scimitars in their hands. They led me to an inner vestibule, where I was divested of my cloak and shoes and regaled with refreshments. Presently an elderly woman, very richly dressed, accompanied by a number of young girls, approached me, and after the usual salutation, informed me that the Sultana Asseki was ready to see me.

All the walls of the kiosk in which she lives are covered with the most beautiful Persian tiles and the floors are of cedar and sandalwood, which give out the most delicious odor. I advanced through an endless row of bending female slaves, who stood on either side of my path. At the entrance to the apartment in which the sultan's wife condescended to receive me, the elderly lady who had accompanied me all the time made me a profound reverence, and beckoned to two girls to give me their aid; so that I passed into the presence of the sultan's wife leaning upon their shoulders.

The sultana, who is a stout but beautiful young woman, sat upon silk cushions striped with silver, near a latticed window overlooking the sea. Numerous slave women, blazing with jewels, attended upon her, holding fans, pipes for smoking, and many objects of value.

When we had selected from these, the great lady, who rose to receive me, extended her hand and kissed me on the brow, and made me sit at the edge of the divan on which she reclined. She asked many questions concerning our country and our religion, of which she knew nothing whatever, and which I answered as modestly and discreetly as I could. I was surprised to notice, when I had finished my narrative, that the room was full of women, who, impelled by curiosity, had come to see me, and to hear what I had to say.

The sultana now entertained me with an exhibition of dancing girls and music, which was very delectable. When the dancing and music were over, refreshments were served upon trays of solid gold sparkling with jewels. As it was growing late, and I felt afraid to remain longer, lest I should vex Her Highness, I made a motion of rising to leave. She immediately clapped her hands, and several slaves came forward, in obedience to her whispered commands, carrying trays heaped up with beautiful stuffs, and some silver articles of fine workmanship, which the princess pressed me to accept. After the usual salutations the old woman who first escorted me into the imperial presence conducted me out, and I was led from the room in precisely the same manner in which I had entered it, down to the foot of the staircase, where my own attendants awaited me.

Hürrem Sultan

Speech by Polonius
William Shakespeare (c. 1600)

William Shakespeare wrote The Tragedy of Hamlet, Prince of Denmark *sometime between 1599 and 1602. The title character, Hamlet, wants to marry Ophelia, daughter of a royal advisor named Polonius. In this speech, Polonius is giving advice to his son, Laertes, before he leaves for France.*

Yet here, Laertes! aboard, aboard, for shame!
The wind sits in the shoulder of your sail,
And you are stay'd for. There;
    my blessing with thee!
And these few precepts in thy memory
See thou character.
    Give thy thoughts no tongue,
Nor any unproportioned thought his act.
Be thou familiar, but by no means vulgar.
Those friends thou hast,
    and their adoption tried,
Grapple them to thy soul with hoops of steel;
But do not dull thy palm with entertainment
Of each new-hatch'd, unfledged comrade.
    Beware
Of entrance to a quarrel, but being in,
Bear't that the opposed may beware of thee.
Give every man thy ear, but few thy voice;
Take each man's censure,
    but reserve thy judgment.

Costly thy habit as thy purse can buy,
But not express'd in fancy; rich, not gaudy;
For the apparel oft proclaims the man,
And they in France of the
    best rank and station
Are of a most select and
    generous chief in that.
Neither a borrower nor a lender be;
For loan oft loses both itself and friend,
And borrowing dulls the edge of husbandry.
This above all: to thine ownself be true,
And it must follow, as the night the day,
Thou canst not then be false to any man.
Farewell: my blessing season this in thee!

Procession of Characters from Shakespeare's Plays *(Unknown Artist, c. 1840)*

A Daily Exercise for Ladies and Gentlewomen
John Murrel (1617)

This cookbook was published in London so that women could "learne and practice the whole art of making pastes, preserves, marmalades, conserves, tart-stuffes, gellies, breads, sucket candies, cordiall waters, conceits in sugar-workes of several kinds. As also to dry lemons, oranges, or other fruits." Here are a few recipes from that book. Since these instructions are hard to follow, you are on your own if you want to make any of these items! Get permission from a parent if you want to try to make them.

To make Marble Paste, called the Italian Chippe

Take Violets, Cowslips, and Clove-gilliflowers, dry them and beate them to fine powder, mingle them with double refined Sugar, cearsed through a tiffanie or a lawne Sieve. Make it up into Sugar plate, with a little gun dragon steept in Rose water and milke. When you have made your plate, then rowle every piece thinne and lay each upon other, and so rowle them up in round rowles, as you would rowle up a leafe of paper. Then cut it endwaies, and rowle it as thinne as paper, and so it will looke finely speckled like a piece of Marble. In like manner you may make Purslane dishes or trenchers of that stuffe.

Still-Life with Bread and Confectionary
Georg Flegel (German, c. 1625)

To preserve Orenges or Lemonds rindes

Drive off the uttermost skinne of your Orenges with a rasp, cut them in two, and take out the core quite and cleane, and let the pils lie in water three or foure daies. Then boile them tender in six or seaven waters, least their bitternesse be distastfull. Then take them up, and drie them in a very faire cloath, and put them to as much Sugar clarified as will cover them. Let them boile softly over the fire halfe an houre at least, and rest in that sirupe three or foure daies. After that time heat them throughly, and take them out of the sirupe, and strengthen it with fresh Sugar boiled therein halfe an houre. Coole it and being blood-warme, put up your fruit in it.

To make rough red Marmalade of Quinces, commonly called lump-Marmalade, that shall looke as red as any Rubie

Pare ripe and well coloured Peare-quinces, and cut them in pieces like die. Parboile them very tender, or rather reasonably tender in faire water, then powre them into a Colender and let the water runne from them into a cleane Bason. Then straine that water through a strainer into a Posnet. For if there be any gravell in the Quinces, it will be in that water. Then take the weight of the Quinces in double refined Sugar very fine. Put halfe thereof into the Posnet, into the water with it a graine of Muske, a slice or two of Ginger tied in a third, and let it boile covered close, untill you see your Sugar come to the colour of Claret wine. Then uncover it, and take out your Ginger, and so let it boile untill your sirupe begin to consume away. Then take it off the fire, and pomice it with a ladle, and so stirre it and coole it, and it will looke thick like tart-stuffe. Then put in your other halfe of your Sugar, and so let it boile, alway stirring it untill it come from the bottome of the Posnet. Then box it, and it will looke red like a Rubie, the putting of the last Sugar brings it to an orient colour.

To make an excellent Tart-stuffe of Prunes

Put six faire Pippins pared and cored unto two or three pound of Prunes, & a pinte of Claret-wine. Stew them tender, and strain them, season them with Cinamon, Ginger, and Sugar, and a little Rose-water.

To make red Ginger-bread, commonly called Leach-lumbar

Grate and dry two stale Manchets, either by the fire, or in an Oven. Sift them through a Sieve, and put to it Cinamon, Ginger, Sugar, Liquorice, Anis-seed. When you have mingled all this together, boile a pint of red wine, & put in your mingled bread, and stirre it, that it be as thick as a Hastie-pudding. Then take it out, and coole it, and mould it with Cinamon, Ginger, Liquorice, and Anise-seede, and rowle it thinne, and print it with your mould, and dry it in a warme Oven.

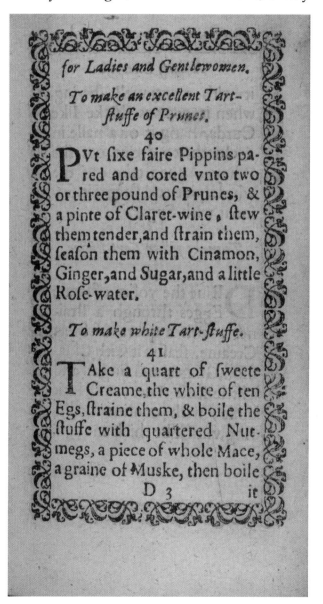

Page from the Daily Exercise *Cookbook*

Letter from William Adams
(1611)

William Adams was born in England in 1564 and became a sailor. In 1598 he joined a Dutch trading expedition with five ships that went to Africa, South America, and finally Japan. Adams was one of the few survivors on the last remaining ship that reached Japan in 1600. Adams wrote a letter in 1611, hoping to get word back to England about his situation. This excerpt is taken from Letters Written by the English Residents in Japan, *edited by N. Murakami and K. Murakawa (1900). The spelling has been modernized.*

So in process of four or five years the Emperor* called me, as several times he had done before. So one time above the rest he would have me to make him a small ship. I answered that I was no carpenter, and had no knowledge thereof. "Well, do your endeavour, saith he: if it be not good, it is no matter."

Wherefore at his command I built him a ship of the burden of eighty tonnes, or there about: which ship being made in all respects as our manner is, he coming aboard to see it, liked it very well; by which means I came in more favour with him, so that I came often in his presence, who from time to time gave me presents, and at length a yearly stipend to live upon, much about seventy ducats by the year, with two pounds of rice a day, daily.

This Dutch map of Japan from 1707 includes a portrayal of William Adams meeting the Japanese Emperor.

Now being in such grace and favour, by reason I learned him some points of geometry, and understanding of the art of mathematics, with other things: I pleased him so, that what I said he would not contrary. At which my former enemies did wonder; and at this time must entreat me to do them a friendship, which to both Spaniards and Portuguese have I done: recompensing them good for evil. So, to pass my time to get my living, it hath cost me great labour and trouble, at the first; but God hath blessed my labour.

In the end of five years, I made supplication to the king to go out of this land, desiring to see my poor wife and children according to conscience and nature. With the which request, the emperor was not well pleased, and would not let me go any more for my country; but to bide in his land. . . .

Therefore I do pray and entreat you in the name of Jesus Christ to do so much as to make my being here in Japan, known to my poor wife: in a manner a widow, and my two children fatherless: which thing only is my greatest grief of heart, and conscience. I am a man not unknown in Ratcliffe and Limehouse, by name to my good Master Nicholas Diggines, and M.

---

* *Adams lived in Japan during the reigns of Tokugawa Ieyasu and Tokugawa Hidetada. This reference is probably to the latter.*

Thomas Best, and M. Nicholas Isaac, and William Isaac, brothers, with many others; also to M. William Jones, and M. Bechet. Therefore may this letter come to any of their hands, or the copy: I do know that compassion and mercy is so, that my friends and kindred shall have news, that I do as yet live in this vale of my sorrowful pilgrimage: the which thing again and again I do desire for Jesus Christ his sake. . . .

Now for my service which I have done and daily do, being employed in the Emperor's service, he hath given me a living, like unto a lordship in England, with eighty or ninety husbandmen,* that be as my slaves or servants: which, or the like precedent, was never here before given to any stranger. Thus God hath provided for me after my great misery; and to him only be all honor and praise, power and glory, both now and for ever, world without end. . . .

This Island of Japan is a great land, and lieth to the northwards, in the latitude of eight and forty degrees, and it lieth east by north, and west by south or west south west, two hundred and twenty English leagues. The people of this Island of Japan are good of nature, courteous above measure, and valiant in war: their justice is severely executed without any partiality upon transgressors of the law. They are governed in great civility. I mean, not a land better governed in the world by civil policy. The people be very superstitious in their religion, and are of divers opinions. There be many Jesuits and Franciscan friars in this land, and they have converted many to be Christians and have many churches in the Island.

Thus, in brief, I am constrained to write, hoping that by one means, or other, in process of time, I shall hear of my wife and children: and so with patience I wait the good will and pleasure of Almighty God. Therefore I do pray all them, or every one of them, that if this my letter shall come to their hands to do the best, that my wife and children, and my good acquaintance may hear of me; by whose good means I may in process of time, before my death hear news, or see some of my friends again. The which thing God turn it to his glory. Amen.

Adams, known in Japan as Anjin Miura, married a Japanese woman and fathered three children. He was instrumental in establishing trade relations between the Japanese and the English. Adams continued to serve the Emperor until Adams' death in 1620. His grave stone in Hirado, Japan, is shown at right. Notice the cross at the top.

---

* *The Emperor had made Adams a samurai.*

"The Tiger, the Brâhman, and the Jackal"
Flora Annie Steel (1894)

Mrs. Steel lived in India with her husband, who was a British official. While her husband did his work in the villages, she spent time with local children, trying to learn folk tales. After hearing the same stories from multiple sources, she compiled them into written form. A collection of these were published in an 1894 book for children called Tales of the Punjab: Told by the People. *The illustration by John Dickson Batten is from another version of the story published by Joseph Jacobs. This particular story is one that different cultures have retold in many forms over the years and around the world.*

Once upon a time a tiger was caught in a trap. He tried in vain to get out through the bars, and rolled and bit with rage and grief when he failed.

By chance a poor Brâhman* came by. "Let me out of this cage, O pious one!" cried the tiger.

"Nay, my friend," replied the Brâhman mildly, "you would probably eat me if I did."

"Not at all!" swore the tiger with many oaths; "on the contrary, I should be for ever grateful, and serve you as a slave!"

Now when the tiger sobbed and sighed and wept and swore, the pious Brâhman's heart softened, and at last he consented to open the door of the cage. Out popped the tiger, and, seizing the poor man, cried, "What a fool you are! What is to prevent my eating you now, for after being cooped up so long I am just terribly hungry!"

In vain the Brâhman pleaded for his life; the most he could gain was a promise to abide by the decision of the first three things he chose to question as to the justice of the tiger's action.

So the Brâhman first asked a pîpal tree what it thought of the matter, but the pîpal tree replied coldly, "What have you to complain about? Don't I give shade and shelter to every one who passes by, and don't they in return tear down my branches to feed their cattle? Don't whimper–be a man!"

Then the Brâhman, sad at heart, went farther afield till he saw a buffalo turning a well-wheel; but he fared no better from it, for it answered, "You are a fool to expect gratitude! Look at me! While I gave milk they fed me on cotton-seed and oil-cake, but now I am dry they yoke me here, and give me refuse as fodder!"

The Brâhman, still more sad, asked the road to give him its opinion.

"My dear sir," said the road, "how foolish you are to expect anything else! Here am I, useful to everybody, yet all, rich and poor, great and small, trample on me as they go past, giving me nothing but the ashes of their pipes and the husks of their grain!"

On this the Brâhman turned back sorrowfully, and on the way he met a jackal, who called out, "Why, what's the matter, Mr. Brâhman? You look as miserable as a fish out of water!"

Then the Brâhman told him all that had occurred. "How very confusing!" said the jackal, when the recital was ended; "would you mind telling me over again? For everything seems so mixed up!"

---

* *A Brâhman (or Brahmin in modern spelling) is a Hindu scholar.*

The Brâhman told it all over again, but the jackal shook his head in a distracted sort of way, and still could not understand.

"It's very odd," said he sadly, "but it all seems to go in at one ear and out at the other! I will go to the place where it all happened, and then perhaps I shall be able to give a judgment."

So they returned to the cage, by which the tiger was waiting for the Brâhman, and sharpening his teeth and claws.

"You've been away a long time!" growled the savage beast, "but now let us begin our dinner."

"Our dinner!" thought the wretched Brâhman, as his knees knocked together with fright; "what a remarkably delicate way of putting it!"

"Give me five minutes, my lord!" he pleaded, "in order that I may explain matters to the jackal here, who is somewhat slow in his wits."

The tiger consented, and the Brâhman began the whole story over again, not missing a single detail, and spinning as long a yarn as possible.

"Oh, my poor brain! oh, my poor brain!" cried the jackal, wringing his paws. "Let me see! how did it all begin? You were in the cage, and the tiger came walking by—"

"Pooh!" interrupted the tiger, "what a fool you are! I was in the cage."

"Of course!" cried the jackal, pretending to tremble with fright; "yes! I was in the cage—no, I wasn't—dear! dear! where are my wits? Let me see—the tiger was in the Brâhman, and the cage came walking by—no, that's not it either! Well, don't mind me, but begin your dinner, for I shall never understand!"

"Yes, you shall!" returned the tiger, in a rage at the jackal's stupidity; "I'll make you understand! Look here—I am the tiger—"

"Yes, my lord!"

"And that is the Brâhman—"

"Yes, my lord!"

"And that is the cage—"

"Yes, my lord!"

"And I was in the cage—do you understand?"

"Yes—no—Please, my lord—"

"Well?" cried the tiger, impatiently.

"Please, my lord!—how did you get in?"

"How!—why, in the usual way, of course!"

"Oh dear me!—my head is beginning to whirl again! Please don't be angry, my lord, but what is the usual way?"

At this the tiger lost patience, and, jumping into the cage, cried, "This way! Now do you understand how it was?"

"Perfectly!" grinned the jackal, as he dexterously shut the door; "and if you will permit me to say so, I think matters will remain as they were!"

The Voyage of François Leguat
François Leguat (1708)

François Leguat was born about 1638. He was a Huguenot who fled France in 1689 to escape persecution. He planned to settle with other Huguenots on the island of Réunion, east of Madagascar in the Indian Ocean (mentioned in Lesson 111). He and several companions ended up having a series of adventures and made a long journey back to Europe. Their trip included a visit to the Cape Colony in South Africa, and Leguat wrote a description in the account of his travels. His narrative was published in 1708. Leguat died in 1735, about age 97. This excerpt is from the English translation edited by Captain Pasfield Oliver in 1891.

Ten Leagues from the Cape up in the Country, there is a Colony call'd Draguestain. It consists of about 300 Souls as well Hollanders as French Protestants, which last fled from France upon revoking the Edict of Nantz.

This Colony extends eight or ten Leagues about, because the Soil not being equally good everywhere, they were fain to cultivate those spots they found to be good, and which occasion'd them to scatter themselves abroad. . . .

They have in this Country a prodigious number of Deer, many Oxen, Sheep, Roe-Bucks, and Apes. There are also Elephants, Rhinoceros's, Elks, Lions, Tigres, Leopards, Wild-Boars, Antilopes, Porcupines, Horses, Asses, Dogs, and Wild-Cats. But the most fierce of these Animals retire into the Country, so soon as the Countrymen begin to till the Ground. The Lions and Tigres are boldest in coming to search for Prey near the Habitations.

As for the Unicorn there is no such sort of Beast. The old and most curious Inhabitants of the Cape, are well satisfy'd with it, and he that made *Caesar's Commentaries* was a Lyar, as well as the rest. The Rhinoceros is the true four-footed Unicorn, for there are Fish, Birds, and some Insects, that have likewise but one Horn. I could heartily wish to have seen one of these Rhinoceros's, by reason of the many Fables that are told of that Beast, as well as of the Crocodiles, and a hundred other Animals. . . .

My Friends that had seen of them, laugh'd at all the Figures the Painters gave of them, and which are here subjoin'd for Curiosities sake. Certainly nothing can be more Comical, than so many pretended Embossings; all which however is fabulous. The true Rhinoceros has a Hide like to that of an Elephant, and the older he is, the more wrinkled he will be: It is the same with us in that Respect. We may very well affirm that the Rhinoceros has but one Horn, in spite of all the fabulous Relations of those we call Naturalists: This Horn is at the extremity of the Nose. He has a sort of Hair in his Tail that is black, as large as a great Knitting-Needle, and harder than Whale-bone. I'll say nothing of Camelions* which are common in this Country, unless that it is not true that they live without eating, which we vulgarly call living upon the Air. They live upon Flies, and such like little Creatures. . . .

The Colony I have been speaking of, which is about ten Leagues from the Cape, has been frequently augmented, and is almost every day, by a considerable number of French

---

* *Chameleons*

Protestants. The Company* maintains a Minister and Reader for them, and affords them every day some fresh Tokens of their Respect.

I was told, if I remember well, while I was with those good People, that the Pastor of this Church, a very honest and sensible Man, was making a new Translation of the Psalms in Verse, or at least correcting, to the best of his Power, that of Marot and Beza to render those sacred Pages more intelligible . . .

Every one must easily conceive there are no beginnings without Difficulties, and our honest Countrymen did not meet with a few at first, but then they were charitably reliev'd, as I have already observ'd, and at length God was pleas'd so to bless their Labours, that they are at present perfectly at ease, nay, some of them are become very Rich. . . .

All this consider'd, 'tis certain the Cape is an extraordinary Refuge for the poor French Protestants. They there peaceably enjoy their Happiness and live in good Correspondence with the Hollanders, who, as every one knows, are of a frank and down-right Humour.

The Pastor mentioned here is Pierre Simond. He and his wife Anne served the Huguenots in South Africa from 1688 to 1700. His French translation of the Psalms may be the first book written in South Africa. Published in Amsterdam in 1704, the English translation of the title is The Africa Night Watches *or* The Psalms of David in French Verse Form. *The Huguenot Monument in Franschhoek, South Africa, was completed in 1945. Pictured below, it commemorates Huguenot influence in that country.*

---

* *The Dutch East India Company*

With the Tibetans in Tent and Temple
Dr. Susie C. Rijnhart (1901)

Petrus and Susie Rijnhart went to Western China and Tibet in 1895 with another missionary, William Ferguson, to share the gospel with the people. Providing medical care gave them opportunities to get to know and love the people. Though this was written several centuries after the time period discussed in the lesson, it provides a look at Tibetan culture and the motivation of Christians to share good news. In this first excerpt, Dr. Rijnhart (the wife) describes a Buddhist religious ceremony.

Tibetan Men

Through our friendship with Ishinima[*] we gained a knowledge of Kumbum[**] and all that pertained to it, which otherwise we might long have sought in vain. Shortly after our visit to his home he accompanied us again to the lamasery to witness an elaborate ceremony on the occasion of the ordination of the priest who was to serve as lamasery doctor. Ishinima having some scruples about appearing publicly as our guide, walked about fifty yards ahead of us, never, however, turning a corner until he assured himself that we were following. Having arrived in the courtyard of the temple where the ceremony was to be held, we took our places, Ishinima standing at some distance opposite us and scarcely taking his eye off us from first to last.

The walls of the temple court were hung with all manner of fantastic pictures executed in flaming colors by Chinese artists. In the middle of the enclosure was a long narrow table, similar to those often found on American picnic grounds, on which were placed rows of decorated plates and brazen vessels of various shapes and sizes, containing tsampa, rice, barley, flour, bread, oil and other eatables. These, we learned, were offerings which had been brought to be sacrificed in honor of the new candidate for the position of medical superintendent. A large crowd of spectators had congregated and were gazing with reverent and longing looks upon the feast prepared for the gods, when suddenly a procession of about fifty lamas broke into the courtyard, arrayed in red and yellow robes, each one carrying in his hand a bell.

As soon as they had seated themselves on the stone pavement, the *mamba fuyeh*, or medical buddha, came in and took his place on an elevated wooden throne covered with crimson and yellow cloth. He wore a tall, handsomely embroidered hat and brilliant ceremonial robes, befitting the occasion. The ceremony began by a deafening clatter of discordant bells, each lama vying with the others to produce the most noise from his instrument. The music was followed by the muttering of some cabalistic incantations and the weird chanting of prayers. Immediately in front of the *mamba fuyeh* was a large urn in the bottom of which a fire was smoldering, sending up its vapory clouds of smoke and incense.

[*] *Their language tutor.*
[**] *A Buddhist monastery. Dr. Rijnhart uses the word lamasery to refer to it. A lama is a Buddhist religious leader in Tibet.*

At a given signal some of the lamas rose and, each one taking up in a ladle a portion of the delicious viands that stood on the table, walked gravely to the urn and dropped it into the fire as an offering in honor of the new *mamba fuyeh*, and finally a stream of liquid which we took to be some kind of holy oil was poured in from a little brass pot. Then there were repetitions of the prayers, incantations and bell-ringing, and it was a long time ere the *mamba fuyeh* was declared duly installed. The position of medical lama is considered one of great importance. The office in the Kumbum lamasery is held for varying periods of time, depending partly on the incumbent's efficiency, but more perhaps on the number of his influential friends. . . .

During a period of fighting between opposing groups, Dr. Rijnhart explains:

In the midst of these stirring times when thoughts of murder and revenge were uppermost in the people's minds, we endeavored to carry on the work of preaching and teaching as well as of healing. The abbot's invitation to reside in the lamasery we could but interpret as a divine call to a larger field of usefulness, and the influence which his patronage gave us in the eyes of the people was but another name for opportunity—a sacred trust for which we felt we should be held responsible. Priests and laymen, women and children, rallied round us, consulting us in their difficulties and giving us every evidence of their trust in us. One of the most encouraging features of our missionary work

Tibetan House

was the Bible School, which was begun soon after our removal to the lamasery, and held every Wednesday and Sunday afternoon in our house at Lusar. The children, who had become attached to us, even following us in the street, were easily gathered in and became at once interested in the colored Bible pictures that hung on our walls. . . .

On Christmas of 1895 we gave the children a feast of waffles and milk tea. Some of the women present said that if their people followed our doctrine they would be better, and added that we taught the children only what was good. Mr. Rijnhart spoke much with the lamas about religious matters, losing no opportunity of pressing the Gospel message. Ishinima declared that if the Mohammedans did not come to attack Lusar and Kumbum it would be because we were there and had prayed to the "Heavenly Ruler" to guard us, and to our certain knowledge Ishinima himself laid aside a Buddha idol which he had always taken to bed for protection, and put his trust in the "Heavenly Ruler." . . .

The Rijnhart's son Charlie was born in Tibet. He died at age 14 months from an unknown illness. Mr. Rijnhart was later killed during another time of violence. At the end of her book, Dr. Rijnhart concludes:

Kind Christian friends have questioned our wisdom in entering Tibet. Why not have waited, they ask, until Tibet was opened by "the powers" so that missionaries could go in under government protection? There is much heart in the question but little logic. Christ does not tell his disciples to wait, but to go. We are not to choose conditions, we are to meet them. The early apostles did not wait until the Roman Empire was "opened" before they kindled that fire that "burned to the water's edge all round the Mediterranean," but carrying their lives in their hands they traveled through the cities of Asia Minor, Greece and finally to Rome, delivering their message in the very centers of paganism. Persecutions came upon them from every side, but nothing but death could hinder their progress or silence their message. They went to glorious martyrdom and being dead they have never ceased to speak.

Paul says, "When it was the good pleasure of God . . . to reveal his Son in me, that I might preach Him among the Gentiles, immediately I conferred not with flesh and blood." (Gal. 1:15-16.) Though he knew bonds and imprisonments awaited him in every city, he pursued his great missionary journeys shrinking not from innumerable perils and even glorying in his tribulations. He was willing "not to be bound only, but also to die at Jerusalem for the name of the Lord Jesus" (Acts 21:13), and although he did not court death he elected to go to the very gates of the Imperial City and face the judgment seat of a Caesar, because of his desire to preach Christ even at Rome. Instead of waiting till the countries under the sway of Rome were opened, the apostle went forth in the power of God to open them.

So it has ever been in the history of Christianity. Had the missionaries waited till all countries were ready and willing to receive them, so that they could go forth without danger and sacrifice, England might still have been the home of barbarians, Livingstone's footsteps never would have consecrated the African wilderness, there would have been no Carey in India, the South Sea Islanders would still be sunk in their cannibalism, and the thousands of Christians found in pagan and heathen lands to-day would still be in the darkness and the shadow of death.

Tibet, like other lands, must have the light. The command is "Go preach the Gospel to every creature." The work is great. So great that beside its greatness any sacrifice involved in its accomplishment is small. Mr. Rijnhart frequently gave expression to his one burning ambition to be of service in evangelizing Tibet—whether by his life or his death, he said, did not matter to him. With David Brainerd he could say, "I longed to be a flame of fire, continually glowing in the service of God and building up Christ's kingdom to my latest, my dying moments." Remembering his consecration I too can be strong and say, as I bring the story to a close, "God doeth all things well—the sacrifice was not too great."

Dr. Rijnhart escaped Tibet and went to Canada after her husband's death. She published her story in 1901. The photos in this section are taken from her book, With the Tibetans in Tent and Temple. *Dr. Rijnhart is pictured at right in Tibetan clothing. She returned to Tibet in 1904 and died in 1908.*

Diary of Samuel Pepys
(1666)

Samuel Pepys (1633-1703) was Secretary to the Admiralty under Kings Charles II and James II. He kept a diary from 1660 to 1669 in shorthand. The Rev. John Smith deciphered the diary and published portions of it in 1825. This excerpt from September 1666 is from an 1893 edition of the diary published by Henry B. Wheatley.

2nd (Lord's day). Some of our mayds sitting up late last night to get things ready against our feast to-day, Jane called us up about three in the morning, to tell us of a great fire they saw in the City. So I rose and slipped on my nightgowne, and went to her window, and thought it to be on the backside of Marke-lane at the farthest; but, being unused to such fires as followed, I thought it far enough off; and so went to bed again and to sleep. About seven rose again to dress myself, and there looked out at the window, and saw the fire not so much as it was and further off. So to my closett to set things to rights after yesterday's cleaning. By and by Jane comes and tells me that she hears that above 300 houses have been burned down to-night by the fire we saw, and that it is now burning down all Fish-street, by London Bridge.

So I made myself ready presently, and walked to the Tower, and there got up upon one of the high places, Sir J. Robinson's little son going up with me; and there I did see the houses at that end of the bridge all on fire, and an infinite great fire on this and the other side of the bridge; which, among other people, did trouble me for poor little Michell and our Sarah on the bridge.

So down, with my heart full of trouble, to the Lieutenant of the Tower, who tells me that it begun this morning in the King's baker's house in Pudding-lane, and that it hath burned St. Magnus's Church and most part of Fish-street already. So I down to the water-side, and there got a boat and through bridge, and there saw a lamentable fire. Poor Michell's house, as far as the Old Swan, already burned that way, and the fire running further, that in a very little time it got as far as the Steeleyard, while I was there. Everybody endeavouring to remove their goods, and flinging into the river or bringing them into lighters that layoff; poor people staying in their houses as long as till the very fire touched them, and then running into boats, or clambering from one pair of stairs by the water-side to another.

And among other things, the poor pigeons, I perceive, were loth to leave their houses, but hovered about the windows and balconys till they were, some of them burned, their wings, and fell down. Having staid, and in an hour's time seen the fire: rage every way, and nobody, to my sight, endeavouring to quench it . . . I to White Hall (with a gentleman with me who desired to go off from the Tower, to see the fire, in my boat); to White Hall, and there up to the Kings closett in the Chappell, where people come about me, and did give them an account dismayed them all, and word was carried in to the King. So I was called for, and did tell the King and Duke of Yorke what I saw, and that unless his Majesty did command houses to be pulled down nothing could stop the fire. They seemed much troubled, and the King commanded me to go to my Lord Mayor from him, and command him to spare no houses, but to pull down [buildings] before the fire every way. The Duke of York bid me tell him that if he would have any more soldiers he shall; and so did my Lord Arlington afterwards, as a great secret.

Here meeting, with Captain Cocke, I in his coach, which he lent me, and Creed with me to Paul's, and there walked along Watlingstreet, as well as I could, every creature coming away loaden with goods to save, and here and there sicke people carried away in beds. Extraordinary goods carried in carts and on backs. At last met my Lord Mayor in Canningstreet, like a man spent, with a handkercher about his neck. To the King's message he cried, like a fainting woman, "Lord! what can I do? I am spent: people will not obey me. I have been pulling down houses; but the fire overtakes us faster than we can do it." That he needed no more soldiers; and that, for himself, he must go and refresh himself, having been up all night. So he left me, and I him, and walked home, seeing people all almost distracted, and no manner of means used to quench the fire. The houses, too, so very thick thereabouts, and full of matter for burning, as pitch and tarr, in Thames-street; and warehouses of oyle, and wines, and brandy, and other things. Here I saw Mr. Isaake Houblon, the handsome man, prettily dressed and dirty, at his door at Dowgate, receiving some of his brothers' things, whose houses were on fire; and, as he says, have been removed twice already; and he doubts (as it soon proved) that they must be in a little time removed from his house also, which was a sad consideration. And to see the churches all filling with goods by people who themselves should have been quietly there at this time. . . .

Pepys described what he saw over the next week as the fire spread and was finally contained. On the 7th, he saw "all the towne burned, and a miserable sight of Paul's church; with all the roofs fallen." He is referring to the old St. Paul's Church. The drawing at left shows that church still in ruins several years after the fire.

The Sunday after the fire began, Pepys noted:

9th (Sunday). Up and was trimmed, and sent my brother to Woolwich to my wife, to dine with her. I to church, where our parson made a melancholy but good sermon; and many and most in the church cried, specially the women. The church mighty full; but few of fashion, and most strangers.

Illustrations of the Dodo
(1600s)

Dutch Admiral Jacob van Neck led an expedition that stopped in Mauritius in 1598. A report of the expedition, published in 1601, contained this illustration of Dutch sailors collecting food on the island. In the middle near the left edge is the first known published image of a dodo.

Emperor Rudolph II of the Holy Roman Empire kept two collections of exotic animals. He employed the Flemish artist Jakob Hoefnagel to illustrate the creatures. Hoefnagel's illustration of a dodo, shown at left, is evidently based on a stuffed dodo brought back from the Indian Ocean rather than on a live bird. It is dated circa 1602.

Emperor Jahangir of the Mogul Empire had a large collection of animals and birds. Someone brought two dodos from Mauritius to add to his collection. The illustration at left, dated about 1625, is attributed to his court artist Ustad Mansur. The dodo is pictured in the middle.

The painting at right is by Dutch artist Cornelius Saftleven. It is dated about 1638.

Russian Games
(1700s)

These games developed at various times in Russian history as people made up rules and shared them with others.

Gorodki

In this game, a set of small wooden pins are arranged in one of several patterns (resembling a cannon, star, or arrow, for example). Players attempt to knock over the pins by throwing a bat at them. Peter the Great played this game as a young man. The photo at left by Eirik Sundvor shows players in the USSR in 1935.

Lapta

This game is played with a bat and ball by two teams of six players. It involves a server tossing the ball for the hitter, players running to score points, and the defense trying to catch the ball and tag the runners. Peter the Great ordered his guards to play the game as part of their fitness program. Some Russians think that Russian immigrants took the game to the United States, where it inspired the creation of baseball. A modern game of lapta is shown at right.

Birulki

In this game, also known as spillikins, several small objects are put in a pile. Traditionally, the objects included toy furniture and other household objects. Using a special hook, as shown at left, players attempt to remove one object from the pile without moving any other objects. The player who successfully pulls the most objects from the pile is the winner.

Svaika

Players in this game throw a metal spike toward a metal ring lying on the ground. The goal is to have the spike land upright in the middle of the ring. The illustration at right is from about 1800.

Letter to Georg Erdmann
Johann Sebastian Bach (1730)

Johann Sebastian Bach was not entirely happy with his position in Leipzig. Local officials criticized him for not giving his duties his full attention, while Bach felt that his talents were not fully appreciated. Bach had attended school with Georg Erdmann, who was serving in Gdansk as a Court Councillor to the Russian Emperor. Bach wrote this letter to Erdmann, seeking help in finding another position. Since Bach continued to work in Leipzig, Erdmann was evidently not able to help him. This text of the letter is from Ernest Newman's translation of Albert Schweitzer's 1908 biography J. S. Bach.

Honoured Sir,

Your Excellency will excuse an old and faithful servant for taking the liberty to trouble you with this letter. Nearly four years have now flown by since your Excellency honoured me with a gracious answer to the letter I sent you, but as I remember that you graciously wished me to give you some news of my vicissitudes, I shall now most obediently proceed to do so.

From my youth up my history has been well known to you, until the change which took me as Kapellmeister to Cothen. There lived there a gracious Prince, who both loved and understood music, and with whom I thought to live the rest of my days. It so happened, however, that his Serene Highness married a Princess of Berenburg, and then it seemed as if the musical inclination of the said Prince had grown a little lukewarm, while at the same time the new Princess appeared to be an amusement to him; so God willed it that I should be called to this place as Director Musices and cantor at St. Thomas's school.

At first it was not wholly agreeable to me to become a cantor after having been a Kapellmeister, on which account I delayed making a decision for a quarter of a year; however, this post was described to me in such favourable terms that finally—especially as my sons seemed inclined towards study,—I ventured upon it in the name of the Most High, and betook myself to Leipzig, passed my examination, and then made the move. Here, by God's will, I am to this day.

But now, since I find (1) that the appointment here is not nearly so considerable as I was led to understand, (2) that it has been deprived of many perquisites, (3) that the town is very dear to live in,* and (4) that the authorities are strange people, with little devotion to music, so that I have to endure almost constant vexation, envy, and persecution, I feel compelled to seek, with the Almighty's aid, my fortune elsewhere. Should your Excellency know of, or be able to find, a suitable appointment in your town for an old and faithful servant, I humbly beg you to give me your gracious recommendation thereto; on my part I will not fail, by using my best diligence, to give satisfaction and justify your kind recommendation and intercession.

My position here is worth about 700 thalers, and when there are rather more funerals than usual the perquisites increase proportionately; but if the air is healthy the fees decrease, last year, for example, being more than 100 thalers below the average from funerals. In Thuringia

---

* In this usage, "dear" means expensive.

I can make 400 thalers go further than twice as many here, on account of the excessive cost of living.

And now I must tell you a little about my domestic circumstances. I am married for the second time, my first wife having died in Cothen. Of the first marriage, three sons and a daughter are still living, whom your Excellency saw in Weimar, as you may be graciously pleased to remember. Of the second marriage, one son and two daughters are living. My eldest son is *Studiosus Juris,** the other two are one in the first and the other in the second class, and the eldest daughter is still unmarried. The children of the other marriage are still little, the eldest, a boy, being six years old. They are one and all born musicians, and I can assure you that I can already form a concert, vocal and instrumental, with my family, especially as my wife sings a good soprano, and my eldest daughter joins in, quite well.

I should almost overstep the bounds of politeness by troubling your Excellency with any more, so I hasten to conclude with all devoted respects, and remain your Excellency's life-long most obedient and humble servant,

Joh. Seb. Bach,
Leipzig, 28th October 1730.

J. S. Bach and His Family at Morning Prayers
Toby Edward Rosenthal (American, 1870)

---

* *This means law student. Wilhelm Friedemann Bach went on to work as a musician.*

Moravian Missionaries
(1700s)

In 1731 Count Zinzendorf met a slave named Antony Ulrich from the Caribbean island of St. Thomas who had been brought to Denmark. Antony had become a Christian and longed for someone to go to St. Thomas to share the gospel with his family. When Zinzendorf shared Antony's appeal with the Brethren, several young men volunteered to go. In 1732 Leonard Dober and David Nitschmann went to Copenhagen to find a ship to take them to St. Thomas. They faced opposition from the Danish officials at first, but eventually they were allowed to leave. This account is from J. E. Hutton's History of the Moravian Church, *published in 1909.*

At Copenhagen, where they called at the court, they created quite a sensation. . . . For a while they met with violent opposition. Von Plesz, the King's Chamberlain, asked them how they would live.

"We shall work," replied Nitschmann, "as slaves among the slaves."

"But," said Von Plesz, "that is impossible. It will not be allowed. No white man ever works as a slave."

"Very well," replied Nitschmann, "I am a carpenter, and will ply my trade."

"But what will the potter do?"

"He will help me in my work."

"If you go on like that," exclaimed the Chamberlain, "you will stand your ground the wide world over."

The first thing was to stand their ground at Copenhagen. As the directors of the Danish West Indian Company refused to grant them a passage out they had now to wait for any vessel that might be sailing. The whole Court was soon on their side. The Queen expressed her good wishes. The Princess Amalie gave them some money and a Dutch Bible. The Chamberlain slipped some coins into Nitschmann's pocket. The Court Physician gave them a spring lancet, and showed them how to open a vein. The Court Chaplain espoused their cause, and the Royal Cupbearer found them a ship on the point of sailing for St. Thomas.

As the ship cast anchor in St. Thomas Harbour the Brethren realized for the first time the greatness of their task. There lay the quaint little town of Tappus, its scarlet roofs agleam in the noontide sun; there, along the silver beach, they saw the yellowing rocks; and there, beyond, the soft green hills were limned against the azure sky. There, in a word, lay the favoured isle, the "First Love of Moravian Missions." Again the text for the day was prophetic: "The Lord of Hosts," ran the gladdening watchword, "mustereth the host of the battle." As the Brethren stepped ashore next day they opened a new chapter in the history of modern Christianity. They were the founders of Christian work among the slaves. For fifty years the Moravian Brethren laboured in the West Indies without any aid from any other religious denomination. They established churches in St. Thomas, in St. Croix, in St. John's, in Jamaica, in Antigua, in Barbados, and in St. Kitts. They had 13,000 baptized converts before a missionary from any other Church arrived on the scene.

Military Instructions to His Generals
Frederick II (c. 1750)

Frederick wrote a volume of military instructions between the War of Austrian Succession (1740-1748) and the Seven Years' War (1756-1763). This excerpt is taken from the 1797 English translation by T. Foster, a British military officer.

Though my country be well peopled, it is doubtful if many men are to be met with of the height of my soldiers: and supposing ever that there was no want of them, could they be disciplined in an instant? It therefore becomes one of the most essential duties of generals who command armies or detachments, to prevent desertion. This is to be effected,

1. By not encamping too near a wood or forest, unless sufficient reason require it.

2. By calling the roll frequently every day.

3. By often sending out patroles of hussars,* to scour the country round about the camp.

4. By placing chasseurs** in the corn by night, and doubling the cavalry posts at dusk to strengthen the chain.

5. By not allowing the soldiers to wander about, and taking care that each troop be led regularly to water and forage by an officer.

6. By punishing all marauding with severity, as it gives rise to every species of disorder and irregularity.

7. By not drawing in the guards, who are placed in the villages on marching days, until the troops are under arms.

8. By forbidding, under the strictest injunctions, that any soldier on a march quit his rank or his division.

9. By avoiding night-marches, unless obliged by necessity.

10. By pushing forward patroles of hussars to the right and left, whilst the infantry are passing through a wood.

continued

---

* *a type of cavalry (soldiers who ride on horses)*
** *lightly-armed soldiers or guards*

11. By placing officers at each end of a defile,[*] to oblige the soldiers to fall into their proper places.

12. By concealing from the soldier any retrograde movement[**] which you may be obliged to make, or giving some specious flattering pretext for doing so.

13. By paying great attention to the regular issue of necessary subsistence, and taking care that the troops be furnished with bread, flesh, beer, brandy, &c.

14. By searching for the cause of the evil, when desertion shall have crept into a regiment or company: enquiring if the soldier has received his bounty and other customary indulgencies, and if there has been no misconduct on the part of the captain. No relaxation of discipline is however on any account to be permitted. It may be said, that the colonel will take care of this business, but his efforts alone cannot be sufficient; for in an army, every individual part of it should aim at perfection, to make it appear to be the work of only one man.

Attack of Prussian Infantry, June 4, 1745
Carl Röchling (German, c. 1910)

---

[*] *a gorge or narrow passage between mountains*
[**] *retreat*

Memoirs of the Court of Marie Antoinette, Queen of France

Jeanne Louise Henriette Campan (1823)

Madame Campan (1752-1822) began serving in the court of King Louis XV at the age of fifteen as a reader for his daughters. She became a lady-in-waiting to Marie Antoinette in 1770 upon Marie's marriage to the king's grandson, the future Louis XVI. Near the end of his life, the controversial philosopher Voltaire wanted to return to Paris. Volatire's criticism of Christianity made Louis XVI unsure about welcoming him openly. Madame Campan recorded this account of the royal attitude toward Voltaire.

In the winter of 1778 the King's permission for the return of Voltaire, after an absence of twenty-seven years, was obtained. A few strict persons considered this concession on the part of the Court very injudicious. The Emperor, on leaving France, passed by the Chateau of Ferney without stopping there. He had advised the Queen not to suffer Voltaire to be presented to her. A lady belonging to the Court learned the Emperor's opinion on that point, and reproached him with his want of enthusiasm towards the greatest genius of the age. He replied that for the good of the people he should always endeavour to profit by the knowledge of the philosophers; but that his own business of sovereign would always prevent his ranking himself amongst that sect. The clergy also took steps to hinder Voltaire's appearance at Court. Paris, however, carried to the highest pitch the honours and enthusiasm shown to the great poet.

It was very unwise to let Paris pronounce with such transport an opinion so opposite to that of the Court. This was pointed out to the Queen, and she was told that, without conferring on Voltaire the honour of a presentation, she might see him in the State apartments. She was not averse to following this advice, and appeared embarrassed solely about what she should say to him. She was recommended to talk about nothing but the "Henriade," "Merope," and "Zaira."* The Queen replied that she would still consult a few other persons in whom she had great confidence. The next day she announced that it was irrevocably decided Voltaire should not see any member of the royal family,—his writings being too antagonistic to religion and morals. "It is, however, strange," said the Queen, "that while we refuse to admit Voltaire into our presence as the leader of philosophical writers, the Marechale de Mouchy should have presented to me some years ago Madame Geoffrin, who owed her celebrity to the title of foster-mother of the philosophers."**

Rejection of faith in God, which Voltaire encouraged, led to terrible suffering for the people of France during the French Revolution, which came a few years later.

---

* *These are poetic and dramatic works by Voltaire.*
** *Marie Thérèse Rodet Geoffrin (1699-1777) hosted regular gatherings for artists and philosophers to discuss their work.*

A Calm Address to Our American Colonies

John Wesley (1775)

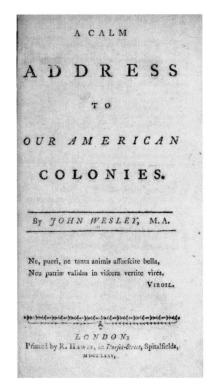

In 1775, as the conflict between England and the American colonies was intensifying, John Wesley published a tract that received wide distribution in England. The title page is shown at left. Wesley expressed his opinion that Englishmen who wanted to overthrow the King were stirring up trouble in America to help their plans. He argued that the Americans already enjoyed religious and political liberty, and that forming a separate country would not help them. Here is an excerpt from Wesley's conclusion:

Brethren, open your eyes! Come to yourselves! Be no longer the dupes of designing men. I do not mean any of your countrymen in America: I doubt whether any of these are in the secret. The designing men, the Ahithophels, are in England; those who have laid their scheme so deep and covered it so well, that thousands who are ripening it, suspect nothing at all of the matter. These well-meaning men, sincerely believing, that they are serving their country, exclaim against grievances, which either never existed, or are aggravated above measure, and thereby inflame the people more and more, to the wish of those who are behind the scene. But be not you duped any longer: do not ruin yourselves for them that owe you no good will, that now employ you only for their own purposes, and in the end will give you no thanks. They love neither England nor America, but play one against the other, in subserviency to their grand design, of overturning the English government. Be warned in time. Stand and consider before it is too late; before you have entailed confusion and misery on your latest posterity. Have pity upon your mother country! Have pity upon your own! Have pity upon yourselves, upon your children, and upon all that are near and dear to you! Let us not bite and devour one another, lest we be consumed one of another! O let us follow after peace! Let us put away our sins; the real ground of all our calamities! Which never will or can be thoroughly removed, till we fear God and honour the king.

Wesley's publication received significant criticism from people in England who supported the American cause. Since England closed American ports in the summer of 1775, not many copies of Wesley's tract reached America. His opinions did become known, however. American Methodists held differing opinions about whether or not the colonies should seek independence. Francis Asbury, one of the leading Methodists in America, expressed disappointment that Wesley had spoken out about American politics, but he maintained his respect for him.

French Art
(1800s)

The Geography Lesson (Portrait of Monsieur Gaudry and His Daughter)
Louis-Léopold Boilly (1803)

The Epsom Derby, *Jean-Louis André Théodore Géricault (1821)*

Nicéphore Niépce created an early method for taking photographs in the 1820s, and he worked with Louis-Jacques-Mandé Daguerre to develop the technology. After Niépce's death in 1833, Daguerre continued to experiment and invented what became known as the daguerreotype. The image below from 1838 captured a scene in Paris. Since the exposure time was at least ten minutes, moving people and carriages are not visible. Two people are captured in the lower left corner, one polishing the other's shoes.

The Old Musician, *Édouard Manet (1862)*

Jean Monet on His Hobby Horse, *Claude Monet (1872). A painting of the artist's son.*

Trade and Travel in the Far East
G. F. Davidson (1846)

G. F. Davidson of Great Britain spent twenty-one years in Java, Singapore, Australia, and China. He published an account of his observations in 1846 after his return to England. This excerpt is from the section about Singapore.

A full description of the inhabitants of Singapore would fill a volume, they are of so many countries. Here may be seen, besides Europeans of different nations, and Americans, the Jew, the Armenian, the Persian, the Parsee, the Arab, the Bengalee, the Malabaree, the China-man, the Malay, the Javanese, the Siamese, the Cochin Chinese, with the native of Borneo, of Macassar, and of every island of the Eastern Archipelago; all in the costumes of their respective countries, and forming motley groupes that can nowhere be surpassed. With the exception of the Europeans, Americans, and Armenians, each class occupies a distinct quarter of the town, mixing but little with the rest, except in business hours, when one and all may be seen in eager converse on the all-important subject of money-making. . . .

The trade of Singapore has, until within the last three years, gone on increasing; but it has now, in the opinion of many people, reached its ultimatum.[*] The harbour is visited regularly by native vessels from all the neighbouring islands, as well as from the Continent; and I shall proceed to notice the nature and value of their trade, respectively, class by class.

And first as to the China junks. These unwieldy vessels visit the Island in numbers varying from one hundred and fifty to two hundred and fifty per annum, their size ranging from fifty to five hundred tons: they are manned and navigated entirely by Chinese. They of course come with the monsoon, and reach Singapore in the months of January, February, and March. Their cargoes form a very material item in the trade of the place, and consist of tea, raw silk, camphor, Nankin (both yellow and blue), immense quantities of coarse earthenware, and supplies of all kinds for the myriads of Chinese that reside on this and the neighbouring islands. . . .

The export cargoes of this class of vessels consist principally of raw cotton, cotton yarn, cotton goods, opium, *béche-de-mer* or sea slug,[**] pepper, tin, rattans, edible birds'-nests, deer-sinews, sharks' fins, fish maws, &c. . . .

The native traders next in importance to the Chinese, are the Bugis. These arrive in October and November, bringing in their uncouth-looking vessels, large quantities of coffee of very good quality, gold-dust, tortoise-shell, native clothes (celebrated all over the Archipelago for their durability), *béche-de-mer*, deer-sinews, rice, &c. . . . On an average, two hundred of these boats come to Singapore in the fall of the year, each manned by about thirty men. . . .

Next in importance to the Bugis, I may rank the Siamese and Cochin Chinese[***] traders, who arrive at Singapore during the north-east monsoon. The trade of these two countries used to be carried on entirely in junks peculiar to each of them respectively; but the state of things has been

---

[*] *The author had this opinion because of the creation of the British colony at Hong Kong in 1843.*
[**] *A reference to the sea cucumber, considered a delicacy in Southeast Asia.*
[***] *From what is now southern Vietnam*

108

materially altered of late. The sovereigns of Siam and Cochin China have recently built and fitted-out several square-rigged vessels, those of Siam being commanded by Europeans, and manned by natives of that country. These vessels are the private property of the kings whose flags they bear, and are loaded on their account and at their risk. Their cargoes consist principally of sugar and rice, which find ready purchasers in Singapore. The sugar of Siam is of very superior quality, and is sent

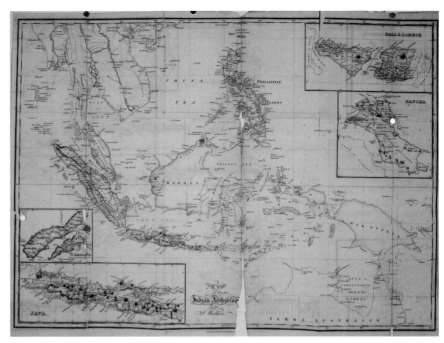

This 1820 map by John Crawfurd shows Southeast Asia, the Malay Archipelago, and Northern Australia.

up in large quantities to Bombay, whence it finds its way up the Indus and the Persian Gulf. The rice of Siam is a superior article, and has of late been sent in considerable quantities to London. The grain is liable to the disadvantage of not keeping so well as that of Bengal or Java; but this fault might, I think, be obviated, partially at all events, by adopting the Calcutta plan of putting a pound or two of rice-dust and lime into each bag: this not only tends to preserve the rice, but repels the destructive weavil; a little black insect that makes its appearance in wheat and rice, in immense numbers, in those warm latitudes.

The Cochin Chinese ships generally bring each four thousand peculs* of sugar, which is of three qualities; namely, sixteen hundred peculs of first quality, the same quantity of second, and eight hundred peculs of the third sort. The first two are good articles, though not equal to the sugars of Siam. The cargoes of these ships are so carefully put up, that I have purchased and re-shipped them without opening or weighing more than five bags out of each hundred, and have never had cause to repent the confidence thus placed in the seller, who is an employé of His Cochin Chinese Majesty. In addition to sugar and rice, the Siamese vessels bring gamboge and cocoa-nut oil of a superior quality: the former is bought up for the London and Continental markets, and the latter for consumption in the Straits' settlements. . . .

Singapore is a free port; and vessels of all kinds and from all nations come and go, without paying one penny to Government in any shape. All that is required of them is, to give in a list of the goods they either land or ship. This regulation is intended to enable the authorities to keep a correct statement of the trade of the place; but it is, I am sorry to add, often evaded by ship-masters and their consignees, who seem to think that no trade can be profitably conducted without a certain portion of mystery attaching to it.

---

* *The pecul (or picul) is an Asian unit of weight, referring to the amount one man can carry on a shoulder pole.*

Constitution of Hayti

(1805)

Toussaint L'Ouverture created the first Constitution of Haiti in 1801. The French government refused to acknowledge that document, and conflict continued. After Haiti (spelled Hayti at the time) gained its independence in 1804, the leaders created a new constitution. Here is an excerpt, as published in the New York Evening Post *in 1805.*

We, H. Christophe, Clerveaux, Vernet, Gabart, Petion, Geffard, Toussaint, Brave, Raphael, Roamin, Lalondridie, Capoix, Magny, Daut, Conge, Magloire, Ambrose, Yayou, Jean Louis Franchois, Gerin, Mereau, Fervu, Bavelais, Martial Besse…

As well in our name as in that of the people of Hayti, who have legally constituted us faithfully organs and interpreters of their will, in presence of the Supreme Being, before whom all mankind are equal, and who has scattered so many species of creatures on the surface of the earth for the purpose of manifesting his glory and his power by the diversity of his works, in the presence of all nature by whom we have been so unjustly and for so long a time considered as outcast children.

Do declare that the tenor of the present constitution is the free, spontaneous, and invariable expression of our hearts, and the general will of our constituents, and we submit it to the sanction of H.M. the Emperor Jacques Dessalines our deliverer, to receive its speedy and entire execution.

Preliminary Declaration.

Art. 1. The people inhabiting the island formerly called St. Domingo, hereby agree to form themselves into a free state sovereign and independent of any other power in the universe, under the name of empire of Hayti.

2. Slavery is forever abolished.

3. The Citizens of Hayti are brothers at home; equality in the eyes of the law is incontestably acknowledged, and there cannot exist any titles, advantages, or privileges, other than those necessarily resulting from the consideration and reward of services rendered to liberty and independence.

4. The law is the same to all, whether it punishes, or whether it protects.

5. The law has no retroactive effect.

6. Property is sacred, its violation shall be severely prosecuted.

7. The quality of citizen of Hayti is lost by emigration and naturalization in foreign countries and condemnation to corporal or disgrace punishments. The first case carries with it the punishment of death and confiscation of property.

8. The quality of Citizen is suspended in consequence of bankruptcies and failures.

9. No person is worthy of being a Haitian who is not a good father, a good son, a good husband, and especially a good soldier.

10. Fathers and mothers are not permitted to disinherit their children.

11. Every Citizen must possess a mechanic art.

12. No whiteman of whatever nation he may be, shall put his foot on this territory with the title of master or proprietor, neither shall he in future acquire any property therein.

13. The preceding article cannot in the smallest degree affect white women who have been naturalized Haytians by Government, nor does it extend to children already born, or that may be born of the said women. The Germans and Polanders naturalized by government are also comprized in the dispositions of the present article. . . .

Haitians began constructing the Citadelle Laferrière in 1805, one of three major forts. Haitian leaders anticipated further French attacks on the new country, but these attacks never came.

Amazing Grace
John Newton (1779)

John Newton and fellow poet William Cowper published a collection of 348 hymns in 1779. This collection, called the Olney Hymns, became popular in both Britain and America. The most famous song from this collection is "Amazing Grace." The photos at right show the song in the original hymnbook.

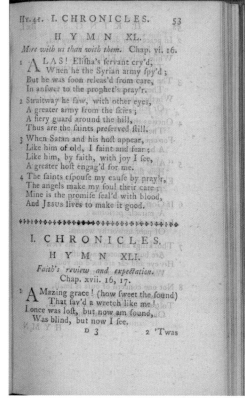

Amazing grace! (how sweet the sound)
   That sav'd a wretch like me!
I once was lost, but now am found,
   Was blind, but now I see.

'Twas grace that taught my heart to fear,
   And grace my fears reliev'd;
How precious did that grace appear
   The hour I first believ'd!

Thro' many dangers, toils, and snares,
   I have already come;
'Tis grace hath brought me safe thus far,
   And grace will lead me home.

The Lord has promis'd good to me,
   His word my hope secures;
He will my shield and portion be
   As long as life endures.

Yes, when this flesh and heart shall fail,
   And mortal life shall cease;
I shall possess, within the veil,
   A life of joy and peace.

The earth shall soon dissolve like snow,
   The sun forbear to shine;
But God, who call'd me here below,
   Will be forever mine.

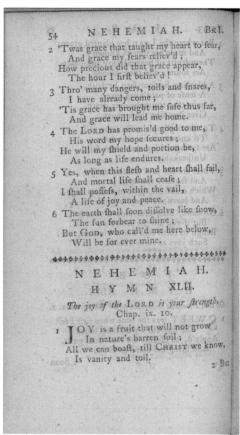

Journals of David Livingstone
(1872)

David Livingstone (1813-1873) spent many years in Africa as a medical missionary and explorer. He did not want Europeans to take over and dominate the native populations. Instead Livingstone believed that the influence of sincere Christians in Africa could encourage education, end the slave trade, and lead to greater prosperity. His journals cover a wide variety of topics, as shown in the following excerpts.

1st August, 1872.—A large party of Baganda have come to see what is stopping the way to Mtesa, about ten headmen and their followers; but they were told by an Arab in Usui that the war with Mirambo was over. About seventy of them come on here to-morrow, only to be despatched back to fetch all the Baganda in Usui, to aid in fighting Mirambo. It is proposed to take a stockade near the central one, and therein build a battery for the cannon, which seems a wise measure. These arrivals are a poor, slave-looking people, clad in bark-cloth, "Mbuzu," and having shields with a boss in the centre, round, and about the size of the ancient Highlanders' targe, but made of reeds. The Baganda already here said that most of the new-comers were slaves, and would be sold for cloths. Extolling the size of Mtesa's country, they say it would take a year to go across it. When I joked them about it, they explained that a year meant five months, three of rain, two of dry, then rain again. Went over to apply medicine to Nkasiwa's neck to heal the outside; the inside is benefited somewhat, but the power will probably remain incomplete, as it now is.

3rd August, 1872.—Visited Salem bin Seff, who is ill of fever. They are hospitable men. Called on Sultan bin Ali and home. It is he who effected the flight of all the Baganda pagazi, by giving ten strings of beads to Motusi to go and spread a panic among them by night; all bolted.

4th August, 1872.—Wearisome waiting, and the sun is now rainy at mid-day, and will become hotter right on to the hot season in November, but this delay may be all for the best.

5th August, 1872.—Visited Nkasiwa, and recommended shampooing the disabled limbs with oil or flour. He says that the pain is removed. More Baganda have come to Kwihara, and will be used for the Mirambo war.

In many parts one is struck by the fact of the children having so few games. Life is a serious business, and amusement is derived from imitating the vocations of the parents—hut building, making little gardens, bows and arrows, shields and spears. Elsewhere boys are very ingenious little fellows, and have several games; they also shoot birds with bows, and teach captured linnets to sing. They are expert in making guns and traps for small birds, and in making and using bird-lime. They make play guns of reed, which go off with a trigger and spring, with a cloud of ashes for smoke. Sometimes they make double-barrelled guns of clay, and have cotton-fluff as smoke. The boys shoot locusts with small toy guns very cleverly. A couple of rufous, brown-headed, and dirty speckle-breasted swallows appeared to-day for the first time this season, and lighted on the ground. This is the kind that builds here in houses, and as far south as Shupanga, on the Zambesi, and at Kuraman. Sun-birds visit a mass of spiders' web to-day; they pick out the young spiders. Nectar is but part of their food. The insects in or at the nectar could not be separated, and hence have been made an essential part of their diet. On closer inspection, however, I see that whilst seeming to pick out young spiders—and they probably do so—they end in detaching the outer coating of spiders' web from the inner stiff paper web, in order to make a nest between the two. The outer part is a thin coating of loose threads: the inner is tough paper, impervious web, just like that which forms the wasps' hive, but stronger. The hen brings fine fibres and places them round a hole 1-1/2 inch in diameter, then works herself in between the two webs and brings cotton to line the inside formed by her body.

—What is the atonement of Christ? It is Himself: it is the inherent and everlasting mercy of God made apparent to human eyes and ears. The everlasting love was disclosed by our Lord's life and death. It showed that God forgives, because He loves to forgive. He works by smiles if possible, if not by frowns; pain is only a means of enforcing love.

If we speak of strength, lo! He is strong. The Almighty; the Over Power; the Mind of the Universe. The heart thrills at the idea of His greatness.

—All the great among men have been remarkable at once for the grasp and minuteness of their knowledge. Great astronomers seem to know every iota of the Knowable. The Great Duke, when at the head of armies, could give all the particulars to be observed in a cavalry charge, and took care to have food ready for all his troops. Men think that greatness consists in lofty indifference to all trivial things. The Grand Llama, sitting in immovable contemplation of nothing, is a good example of what a human mind would regard as majesty; but the Gospels reveal Jesus, the manifestation of the blessed God over all as minute in His care of all. He exercises a vigilance more constant, complete, and comprehensive, every hour and every minute, over each of His people than their utmost selflove could ever attain. His tender love is more exquisite than a mother's heart can feel.

6th August, 1872.—Wagtails begin to discard their young, which feed themselves. I can think of nothing but "when will these men come?" Sixty days was the period named, now it is eighty-four. It may be all for the best, in the good Providence of the Most High.

9th August, 1872.—I do most devoutly thank the Lord for His goodness in bringing my men near to this. Three came to-day, and how thankful I am I cannot express. It is well—the men who went with Mr. Stanley came again to me. "Bless the Lord, my soul, and all that is within me, bless His holy name." Amen.

Letter to W. J. P. Burton
Florence Nightingale (1897)

Florence Nightingale's family home in England was called Lea Hurst. After she moved away, Florence maintained an interest in the nearby Lea Board School. She frequently corresponded with Mr. Burton, who became master at the school in 1888.

Aug. 30/97
10, South Street
Park Lane. W.

Dear Mr. Burton

I am delighted to hear the result of the School Scripture Examination - not that a Scripture Examination ensures an earnest life necessarily among the children, any more than a Grammar Examination. But it is a Master's (or a Mother's) <u>daily</u> Scripture lesson, from which the children learn whether he (or she) means it for their <u>life</u> or no - whether it is to bring in "the kingdom" into our lives, or whether it is merely a lesson in words.

I am sure yours are not merely lessons in <u>words</u> - but that you look to their future lives as e.g. - Dr. Arnold of Rugby did, & Mr. Jowett, the Master of Balliol College Oxford, (who is dead) did to the future lives of his undergraduates.

I have not written - from the press of work which has not left me a moment. But Lea Board School is always in my thoughts.

Yours sincerely
F. Nightingale

Excuse pencil

Mrs. Shore Nightingale is just coming back from Germany & Belgium.

Japanese Art

Three Beauties of the Present Day, *Utamaro* (*c. 1793*)

South Wind, Clear Sky, *Katsushika Hokusai (c. 1830)*

Lakeside, *Kuroda Seiki (1897)*

This image is Foreign Ships Calling at Port *by Hiroshige Utagawa (c. 1860). It was printed as a part of a popular Japanese game called* sugoroku, *in which players used dice to move around the board.*

Gold, Gold, Gold!
W. H. Lang (1900)

This excerpt is from a history of Australia published by William Henry Lang.

The Australian diggings became the magnet which seemed to be attracting the whole earth. Even her own towns were deserted. Servants were not to be had at any wage. Doctors, lawyers, shoeblacks, coachbuilders, butchers and bakers—everybody—rushed away to the diggings, eager to be rich. The newspapers were full of nothing else but gold, news-sheets, and advertisements.

Parramatta, a suburb of Sydney, was absolutely depopulated. It was a mad time. When Hargraves* had completed his bargain with Government, he again started out on horseback for the fields. He found a stream of people going both ways, out to the diggings and back again. Those going out were full of hope and fire, their faces shining like those travelers in the "Pilgrim's Progress" who were going up to the Golden City. Those coming back were moving along slowly, sullen and sulky—beaten.

It was like the two streams of fighters which eye-witnesses described as going up and down Spion Kop in the Boer War. Those disappointed ones were vowing a terrible vengeance on him who had deceived them, as they called it. Hargraves did not tell them who he was. But at a ferry, where numbers had to wait their turn to be taken over, having first mounted his horse, he made a speech to the discontented, pointing out how and why they had failed. It was as well that he had been wise enough to mount his horse before he disclosed his name. The crowd would have lynched him.

They were a motley crew, both coming and going. There was even a blind man being led by a lame one. The cripple extended his hand over his crutch, and the blind one held it, and so they went off with the best of them, all athirst for gold.

There was no difficulty in finding your way. The roads were full of passengers of every kind, on foot, on horseback, in drays and wagons—all sorts. And when you at length reached the land of promise, it was a picturesque sight.

As you topped the last hill in the ranges, the mining township lay at your feet, all made of canvas tents or of wood huts. The creek, on which the gold was being won, wound at the feet of thickly timbered hills, and every here and there was joined by a gully from the mountains.

The smoke was rising blue in the distance, and from far down beneath you arose a constant rumble and hum like distant thunder. It was the noise of the "cradles." Then as evening fell, the lights of innumerable fires began to twinkle through the darkness, the rumble of the cradles ceased, and after a while the township slept.

---

* *Edward Hammond Hargraves moved to Australia after his unsuccessful search for gold in California. He popularized the goldfields of Australia and secured a government position.*

Chinese Games

Chuiwan

A Chinese book written around 1000 describes a game involving digging holes in the ground and hitting balls into them. This painting from the early 1400s shows players using clubs to hit balls toward holes with flags. Its popularity faded during the Ming Dynasty.

Xiangqi

This game is similar to chess. Two players move their pieces on a board. Each is attempting to capture the opponent's general. The other pieces are the advisor, elephant, horse, chariot, cannon, and soldier. Published rules appeared around 800, though the game likely dates back much farther. This photo shows game pieces dated to the Song Dynasty (960-1279).

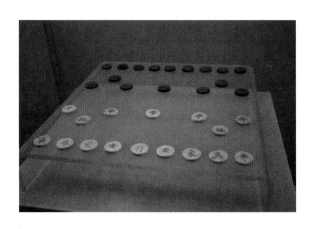

Cuju

Before the time of Christ, Chinese soldiers were playing this game as a military exercise. Players attempted to kick a ball into a small net without using their hands. Over several centuries, its popularity spread among all classes of Chinese society. By the time of the Song Dynasty, professional cuju players were competing in China. This painting by Su Hanchen shows children playing the game (c. 1150).

Go

The game of go originated in China many hundreds of years ago, and it spread to different parts of Asia and later around the world. It remains extremely popular in China. In this game, players alternate placing white and black stones on the board. Each attempts to surround and remove the opponent's pieces. The image at right is cropped from a much larger image of the Ming Court by Qiu Ying (c. 1550).

Touhu

The name of this game is translated literally as "pitch-pot." It also has existed for many hundreds of years. Players attempt to toss arrows or sticks into a large canister. It remained popular in China into the 20th century. The photo shows players in Korea, where the game remains popular.

Mahjong

The Chinese have been playing games using cards and dominoes for many centuries. Mahjong evidently developed in the 1800s using a special set of tiles. The original rules are similar to the card game rummy. In the early 1900s, mahjong became an international phenomenon with different versions appearing in different countries. This 2015 photo shows players in a tearoom in China.

South!

Ernest Shackleton (1919)

Ernest Shackleton (1874-1922) accompanied Robert Scott and Edward Wilson on an expedition to Antarctica in 1901. He led his own expedition from 1907 to 1909 and got to within about 100 miles of the South Pole.

After Roald Amundsen reached the South Pole in 1912, Shackleton developed a plan to cross the continent of Antarctica through the Pole. Shackleton and his men embarked in late 1914. Their ship, Endurance, *became trapped in the ice, as seen in the photo below by Frank Hurley. They were stranded for months.*

Shackleton and five others sailed a small lifeboat across hundreds of miles of stormy ocean to South Georgia Island in the southern Atlantic Ocean. Shackleton, Frank Worseley, and Tom Crean then crossed the mountains and glaciers of the island to reach the whaling station of Stromness. This excerpt from Shackleton's account of the expedition describes their arrival at Stromness.

Cautiously we started down the slope that led to warmth and comfort. The last lap of the journey proved extraordinarily difficult. Vainly we searched for a safe, or a reasonably safe, way down the steep ice-clad mountain-side. The sole possible pathway seemed to be a channel cut by water running from the upland. Down through icy water we followed the course of this stream. We were wet to the waist, shivering, cold, and tired. Presently our ears detected an unwelcome sound that might have been musical under other conditions. It was the splashing of a waterfall, and we were at the wrong end.

When we reached the top of this fall we peered over cautiously and discovered that there was a drop of 25 or 30 ft., with impassable ice-cliffs on both sides. To go up again was scarcely thinkable in our utterly wearied condition. The way down was through the waterfall itself. We made fast one end of our rope to a boulder with some difficulty, due to the fact that the rocks had been worn smooth by the running water. Then Worsley and I lowered Crean, who was the heaviest man. He disappeared altogether in the falling water and came out gasping at the bottom. I went next, sliding down the rope, and Worsley, who was the lightest and most nimble member of the party, came last.

At the bottom of the fall we were able to stand again on dry land. The rope could not be recovered. We had flung down the adze from the top of the fall and also the logbook and the cooker wrapped in one of our blouses. That was all, except our wet clothes, that we brought out of the Antarctic, which we had entered a year and a half before with well-found ship, full equipment, and high hopes. That was all of tangible things; but in memories we were rich. We had pierced the veneer of outside things. We had "suffered, starved, and triumphed, grovelled down yet grasped at glory, grown bigger in the bigness of the whole."* We had seen God in His splendours, heard the text that Nature renders. We had reached the naked soul of man.

Shivering with cold, yet with hearts light and happy, we set off towards the whaling-station, now not more than a mile and a half distant. The difficulties of the journey lay behind us. We tried to straighten ourselves up a bit, for the thought that there might be women at the station made us painfully conscious of our uncivilized appearance. Our beards were long and our hair was matted. We were unwashed and the garments that we had worn for nearly a year without a change were tattered and stained. Three more unpleasant-looking ruffians could hardly have been imagined. Worsley produced several safety-pins from some corner of his garments and effected some temporary repairs that really emphasized his general disrepair.

Down we hurried, and when quite close to the station we met two small boys ten or twelve years of age. I asked these lads where the manager's house was situated. They did not answer. They gave us one look—a comprehensive look that did not need to be repeated. Then they ran from us as fast as their legs would carry them. We reached the outskirts of the station and passed through the "digesting-house," which was dark inside. Emerging at the other end, we met an old man, who started as if he had seen the Devil himself and gave us no time to ask any question. He hurried away. This greeting was not friendly. Then we came to the wharf, where the man in charge stuck to his station. I asked him if Mr. Sorlle (the manager) was in the house. . . .

Mr. Sorlle's hospitality had no bounds. He would scarcely let us wait to remove our freezing boots before he took us into his house and gave us seats in a warm and comfortable room. We were in no condition to sit in anybody's house until we had washed and got into clean clothes, but the kindness of the station-manager was proof even against the unpleasantness of being in a room with us. He gave us coffee and cakes in the Norwegian fashion, and then showed us upstairs to the bathroom, where we shed our rags and scrubbed ourselves luxuriously. . . .

When I look back at those days I have no doubt that Providence guided us, not only across those snowfields, but across the storm-white sea that separated Elephant Island from our landing-place on South Georgia. I know that during that long and racking march of thirty-six hours over the unnamed mountains and glaciers of South Georgia it seemed to me often that we were four, not three. I said nothing to my companions on the point, but afterwards Worsley said to me, "Boss, I had a curious feeling on the march that there was another person with us." Crean confessed to the same idea. One feels "the dearth of human words, the roughness of mortal speech" in trying to describe things intangible, but a record of our journeys would be incomplete without a reference to a subject very near to our hearts.

With help from British and Chilean ships, Shackleton was finally able to rescue the rest of his men who had remained on tiny Elephant Island, near the coast of Antarctica. Shackleton attempted to lead another expedition to the Antarctic in 1921. However, he died en route while on South Georgia Island and was buried there.

---

* *A quotation from "The Call of the Wild," a poem by Robert William Service.*

Fragments of Serbian National Wisdom
Nicholai Velimirovic (1916)

Nicholai Velimirovic, pictured at left, was a leader in the Serbian Orthodox Church. During World War I, he traveled to the United States and England to raise awareness and support for Serbians suffering in the conflict. While he was in England, in 1916, some of his lectures and a collection of Serbian proverbs and poetry were published as the book Serbia in Light and Darkness. *These are some of those collected proverbs.*

Be as patient as an ox, as brave as a lion, as industrious as a bee, and as cheerful as a bird.

Every penny that you give to a beggar, God counts double as His debt to you.

Living, we see the bright side of life and the dark side of death, but afterwards we will see each reversed.

Even the thief pays for what he steals, for in getting an inch of good for his body he loses an inch of his soul.

Man's greatest wisdom is nearer the wisdom of the horse than it is to the wisdom of God.

Construct a better world, and then you may say that this one is bad.

There is no real joy except the joy of a righteous man.

There is no news but what is half old.

God is not hidden, but our eyes are too small to see Him.

By true prayer we confess our sins; by false prayer we report our deeds to God.

When men are quarrelling about the land, God is standing among them and whispering: "I am the Proprietor!"

What is it to be a gentleman? To be the first to thank, and the last to complain.

It is better that your good deed should be forgotten than that your evil deed should make you famous.

Giving is pleasanter than receiving.

Economise in speaking, but not in thinking.

"The Garden in Winter"
L. M. Montgomery (1916)

Lucy Maud Montgomery, pictured at right about 1900, was a Canadian author. She is best known for the Anne of Green Gables *series of books, first published in 1908. In 1916 she published* The Watchman and Other Poems. *The book was dedicated "to the memory of the gallant Canadian soldiers who have laid down their lives for their country and their empire." This is one of her poems.*

Frosty-white and cold it lies
Underneath the fretful skies;
Snowflakes flutter where the red
Banners of the poppies spread,
And the drifts are wide and deep
Where the lilies fell asleep.

But the sunsets o'er it throw
Flame-like splendor, lucent glow,
And the moonshine makes it gleam
Like a wonderland of dream,
And the sharp winds all the day
Pipe and whistle shrilly gay.

Safe beneath the snowdrifts lie
Rainbow buds of by-and-by;
In the long, sweet days of spring
Music of bluebells shall ring,
And its faintly golden cup
Many a primrose will hold up.

Though the winds are keen and chill
Roses' hearts are beating still,
And the garden tranquilly
Dreams of happy hours to be–
In the summer days of blue
All its dreamings will come true.

Rio de Janeiro and the Raising of a Statue
October 23, 1930

The Freeman's Journal, *founded in 1850 by Irish immigrants in Sydney, Australia, was a weekly Catholic publication. This article was published during construction of the statue of Christ the Redeemer.*

Probably Rio de Janeiro is the most beautifully situated capital in all the world, writes an Irish exchange. Conceive Clew Bay magnified enormously and set in tropical waters of blinding blue, with sumptuous verdure clothing the soaring mountains all around—conceive Westport magnified into a vast city, with skyscrapers rising from the water's edge, where great liners lie; that is a faint image of the capital of Brazil. Painters have striven to depict the city and its setting both in golden evening and in glittering night; but travellers assure us that the reality can be conceived but dimly until it is seen in actuality.

Now among the mountains that surround this great capital, there is one high and abrupt peak that rises like a prodigious tower right over the city plain. It is named Corcovado. At this moment it is crowned by a tall frame work of scaffolding, and within that scaffolding may be discerned a growing form in white stone. What is being built? Is it some toy for sight-seers—some tower whence they may view the scene, with a restaurant and a dance hall? No, for Rio de Janiero is a Catholic capital, and it has found a nobler use for that mountain site than frivolity and money-making. That which is being built is a great figure of Christ the Redeemer.

The design has been published and it is a thing of rare beauty. The Divine and pierced Hands are extended as once upon the Cross, but now in a gesture of mercy. The Divine Eyes seem to gaze down upon the teeming city in perfect love. Soon the great statue will be complete, and then that superb scene will be dominated by the sublime image of the Redeemer. Everyone has read of the 'Christ of the Andes'—a similar statue of great magnitude that was erected among the solitary heights of the range that bounds Chile in order to symbolise the lasting peace that has been made between Chile and her neighbor. When we contemplate these great emblems of the Faith, must we not admire the nations that conceive them?

It is a fashion among non-Catholics to speak slightingly of Latin America. The Latin Republics are young and growing States, and their political life sometimes is dashed by the turbulence that older and outworn countries have left behind them. When we read of an exciting manifestation in a South American State, we do well to discount the hostile report, and to remember that those young Republics are Catholic States with a Catholic public life, vast confraternities and spiritual works, pilgrimages, Orders and missions. These are nations that can set the image of Christ the Redeemer in the loftiest site above their cities, when New York sets the image of imaginary Liberty, and Dublin preserves Horatio, Lord Nelson.

Holocaust Memorials

Judenplatz Holocaust Memorial
Rachel Whiteread, 2000
Vienna, Austria

The Last Way
Leonid Levin and Elsa Pollak, 2000
Minsk, Belarus

Stone Flower
Bogdan Bogdanović, 1966
Jasenovac, Croatia

Names of Victims Hand-Written on the
Walls of the Pinkas Synagogue, 1995
Prague, Czech Republic

Memorial at the Site of the
Vaivara Concentration Camp, 1994
Klooga, Estonia

Memorial to the Murdered Jews of Europe
Peter Eisenman and Buro Happold, 2005
Berlin, Germany

Shoes on the Danube Bank
Can Togay, 2005
Budapest, Hungary

Hall of Names at Yad Vashem
Collected from 1950s to the Present
Jerusalem, Israel

New Orleans Holocaust Memorial
Yaacov Agam, 2003
New Orleans, Louisiana, USA

From Boat Person to Bishop
Gisèle Nyembwe and Vincent Nguyen (2010)

TORONTO, Canada, March 12 (United Nations High Commissioner for Refugees) – In January [2010], 43-year-old Vincent Nguyen was ordained as Canada's youngest Roman Catholic bishop and the first of Asian descent. Twenty-seven years earlier, as he stepped onto his uncle's wooden fishing boat on the coast of southern Vietnam, he never imagined he would end up as a leading religious figure in a cosmopolitan city on the other side of the world. He was born and brought up in the Central Highlands town of Ban Me Thuot, which was the scene of a decisive Communist North Vietnamese victory in 1975. Bishop Nguyen, whose great-great grandfather was martyred for his Catholic faith in the 19th Century, decided to flee the country by sea in 1983 so that he would be free to worship. A Japanese freighter picked up his uncle's boat seven days into the trip and took the 20 passengers to Japan, where the young Nguyen spent a year in a refugee camp before being resettled in Toronto. He studied for a degree in electrical engineering before becoming a priest in 1998. The new auxiliary bishop in the Archdiocese of Toronto will represent hundreds of thousands of Canadian Roman Catholics who have immigrated from Asia, Africa and Latin America. Bishop Nguyen reflected on his experience as a refugee in an exchange of e-mails with UNHCR Public Information Assistant Gisèle Nyembwe. Excerpts:

You left Vietnam by boat in 1983. What sticks in your mind from the risky voyage?

Being rescued from a small wooden boat on the ocean is an indescribable experience that I can never forget. We risked our lives on this journey without the certainty that we would make it. We were aware that many people perished during similar journeys . . . We risked our lives in order to find freedom elsewhere. Being rescued also meant that we could start hoping to see our dreams fulfilled. With these feelings and thoughts in my mind, I boarded the [rescue] ship with a great sense of gratitude to those who saved us. Above all, I was grateful to God who carried us through this journey . . . After we boarded the ship, we sang a hymn of thanksgiving. All of us, bar one, were Catholics. I can never forget that moment.

You recently had a big reunion with all your siblings. How did that feel?

When I left Viet Nam, I never thought I would see my family again. The situation in Viet Nam changed with time and I had opportunities to go back and visit them many times. However, the reunion with my entire family at my recent episcopal ordination [in Toronto on January 13] was the first since 1983. I was overwhelmed with joy. In fact, I cried when . . . I started the process of helping them obtain visas to visit Canada.

Today, you are an inspiration for many refugee children. What inspired you as a child?

As a child in a refugee camp, I did not have many responsibilities aside from learning Japanese. I simply enjoyed the freedom and observed others around me doing the same. Later on, I was blessed to be placed at a refugee camp run by the [Canada-based] Sisters of St. Vincent de Paul. Among their many good works, these nuns cared for the poor and disabled. After hours of language study, I accompanied them on their visits and assisted them with their work. It gave me a great sense of service, practising the command of loving others. It was a way for me to give back some of what I had been receiving from others.

Did you have any problems integrating after arriving in Canada?

One of my biggest problems was the English language. At the beginning, it was quite a struggle. I had to take ESL [English as a Second Language] classes in the summer holidays in addition to regular classes during the school year. My progress was very slow. It was not easy. Learning a new language takes time and even though I have been in this country for years, I am still learning.

Has your experience as a refugee had any effect on your religious career?

As a refugee child, I experienced and learned from the goodness of people who cared for those [forcibly] displaced from their homes and countries. This experience in some ways strengthens my belief and trust in God.

What do you think when you read negative stories about refugees?

Surely, there are negative stories and experiences out there. However, should we stop doing good simply because of those stories? We can take measures to ensure that our works effectively and fruitfully help those in need. We should not, however, be discouraged because things do not turn out exactly the way we want. We never know what the fruits of our kindness and good works may be—we might be surprised someday.

Meanwhile, thank you for providing this opportunity for me to say thanks to all the people who helped me and many others when we were refugees. Three years ago, I visited my cousin in Switzerland and passed by the UNHCR head office in Geneva. I asked my cousin to stop so that I could have my picture taken in front of the entrance. The picture was lost when my computer crashed not long after. That, however, shows I remember you all and I am deeply grateful for your efforts in helping me. May God continue to bless you and keep you all in his love.

Bishop Vincent Hieu Nguyen

Indian Home Rule
Mohandas Gandhi (1909)

Gandhi originally wrote this book in his native language of Gujarati. The British banned the original version in India, but they did not ban Gandhi's English translation. Gandhi is pictured at left about the time of writing.

In the book, Gandhi shares thoughts on civilization, technology, religion, and how Indians should live in their own country. In this section he describes his philosophy of passive resistance. As a contrast to physical force, he uses the expression "soul force" to describe the power of love and truth to conquer evil without violence.

The poet Tulsidas has said: "Of religion, pity or love is the root, as egotism of the body. Therefore, we should not abandon pity so long as we are alive."* This appears to me to be a scientific truth. I believe in it as much as I believe in two and two being four. The force of love is the same as the force of the soul or truth. We have evidence of its working at every step. The universe would disappear without the existence of that force. But you ask for historical evidence. It is, therefore, necessary to know what history means. The Gujarati equivalent means: "It so happened." If that is the meaning of history, it is possible to give copious evidence. But if it means the doings of kings and emperors, there can be no evidence of soul-force or passive resistance in such history. You cannot expect silver-ore in a tin-mine.

History, as we know it, is a record of the wars of the world, and so there is a proverb among Englishmen that a nation which has no history, that is, no wars, is a happy nation. How kings played how they become enemies of one another and how they murdered one another is found accurately recorded in history and, if this were all that had happened in the world, it would have been ended long ago. If the story of the universe had commenced with wars, not a man would have been found alive to-day. Those people who have been warred against have disappeared, as, for instance, the natives of Australia, of whom hardly a man was left alive by the intruders. Mark, please, that these natives did not use soul-force in self-defence, and it does not require much foresight to know that the Australians will share the same fate as their victims. "Those that wield the sword shall perish by the sword." With us, the proverb is that professional swimmers will find a watery grave.

The fact that there are so many men still alive in the world shows that it is based not on the force of arms but on the force of truth or love. Therefore the greatest and most unimpeachable evidence of the success of this force is to be found in the fact that, in spite of the wars of the world, it still lives on.

Thousands, indeed, tens of thousands, depend for their existence on a very active working of this force. Little quarrels of millions of families in their daily lives disappear before the exercise of this force. Hundreds of nations live in peace. History does not and cannot take

---

* *Tulsidas was a Hindu philosopher who lived in the 1500s.*

note of this fact. History is really a record of every interruption of the even working of the force of love or of the soul. Two brothers quarrel: one of them repents and re-awakens the love that was lying dormant in him; the two again begin to live in peace: nobody takes note of this. But if the two brothers, through the intervention of solicitors or some other reason, take up arms or go to law—which is another form of the exhibition of brute-force—their doings would be immediately noticed in the press, they would be the talk of their neighbours, and would probably go down to history. And what is true of families and communities is true of nations. There is no reason, to believe that there is one law for families, and another for nations. History, then, is a record of an interruption of the course of nature. Soul-force, being natural, is not noted in history.

Letter to Sarah
C. S. Lewis (1944)

C. S. Lewis received thousands of letters, many of them from children who read his Chronicles of Narnia *series of books. He spent many hours writing replies. He exchanged several letters with his goddaughter Sarah. She was the daughter of one of Lewis' former students. This letter, written during WWII, mentions the issue of food shortages. It is taken from the collection* C. S. Lewis' Letters to Children, *edited by Lyle W. Dorsett and Marjorie Lamp Mead. Reprinted with permission of The CS Lewis Company Ltd.*

July 16, 1944

My dear Sarah—Thank you very much for sending me the pictures of the Fairy King and Queen at tea (or is it breakfast?) in their palace and all the cats (what a lot of cats they have! And a separate table for them. How sensible!). I liked them very much. It must be nice for them (I mean the King and Queen) having so many currants in their cake. We don't get many now, do we? I am getting to be quite friends with an old Rabbit who lives in the Wood at Magdalen.* I pick leaves off the trees for him because he can't reach up to the branches and he eats them out of my hand. One day he stood up on his hind legs and put his front paws against me, he was so greedy. I wrote this about it;

A funny old man had a habit
of giving a leaf to a rabbit.
At first it was shy
But then, by and by,
It got rude and would stand up to grab it.

But it's a very nice Rabbit all the same; I call him "Baron Biscuit." Please tell Mummie I thank her for her nice letter. I didn't have a bad time in the Home but they didn't give me enough to eat and they washed me all over as if I wasn't old enough to wash myself. Have you ever met a hospital-nurse? They are very strong-minded women. No more now because I am still not quite better. Lots of love to you and everyone else

your affectionate godfather
C. S. Lewis

---

* *The name of the college at Oxford University where Lewis taught.*

Day of Mourning Statement
Douglas Nicholls (1938)

The April 1938 issue of The Abo Call *magazine included a summary of the proceedings at the Day of Mourning. It noted that "about 100 persons of Aboriginal blood attended the conference" and that the leaders had received telegrams and letters "from Aborigines all over Australia expressing support." Douglas Nicholls was one of several speakers at the event. The attendees voted unanimously in favor of the resolution shown below.*

Resolution

"We, representing the Aborigines of Australia, assembled in conference at the Australian Hall, Sydney, on the 26th day of January, 1938, this being the 150th Anniversary of the Whiteman's seizure of our country, hereby make protest against the callous treatment of our people by the whitemen during the past 150 years, and we appeal to the Australian nation of today to make new laws for the education and care of Aborigines, we ask for a new policy which will raise our people to full citizen status and equality within the community."

Remarks by Doug Nicholls (Victorian Aborigines League):

On behalf of Victorian Aborigines I want say that we support this resolution in every way. The public does not realise what our people have suffered for 150 years. Aboriginal girls have been sent to Government Reserves and have not been given any opportunity to improve themselves. Their treatment has been disgusting. The white people have nothing for us whatever. Put on reserves, with no proper education, how can Aborigines take their place as equals with whites? Now is our chance to have things altered. We must fight our very hardest in this cause. After 150 years our people are still influenced and bossed by white people. I know that we could proudly hold our own with others if given the chance. Do not let us forget, also, those of our own people who are still in a primitive state. It is for them that we should try to do something. We should all work in cooperation for the progress of Aborigines throughout the Commonwealth.

Speech on Investiture as Governor of South Australia

Douglas Nicholls (1976)

The photo at right shows Douglas Nicholls on December 1, 1976, the day he became the first Aboriginal governor of an Australian state. He made the following remarks.

Your Excellency, the Lieutenant Governor, the Honourable the Chief Justice, the Honourable the Premier, Honourable Ministers, the right Honourable the Lord Mayor, the Honourable the President of the Legislative Council, the Honourable the Speaker of the House of the Assembly, Leaders of the Opposition, distinguished guests, ladies and gentlemen.

Among the very few things I want to say, I want to thank the Premier, the Honourable the Lord Mayor for their welcome here today. On behalf of the people of this state, and as people of South Australia I have already felt the warmth of the people here today and the welcome that has been extended to us.

I stand before you today with mixed feelings. As appointed Governor of South Australia, it's a great honour, not only for Lady Nicholls and I but for the Aboriginal people of Australia. It's a first and a historical first and South Australia leads the way. Nothing new. South Australia was first to grant the franchise to women, was the first state in Australia to appoint a woman as a judge to the Supreme Court in Australia. For many years it added some measure, tackled the question of the Aboriginal problem within this state. Churches of all denominations with the staff of self-sacrificing people. Men and women who left the comforts of home for the dust and flies. Another disability of the inland and we pay tribute to these great people.

I can think of no honour than to hold the commission from Her Majesty the Queen to be Her Majesty's Representative in this state, South Australia. I'll take home the great privilege and honor to be in the position to take and swear the official oath. I am proud of my commission as Governor for the State of South Australia. I am an Aborigine but I'm aware that accepting this appointment as a representative for Her Majesty the Queen in South Australia I have an equal duty towards every citizen of this state regardless of creed or color, youth or age.

International Space Station Blog
NASA (2015)

A blog published by NASA records daily activities of the crew of the International Space Station. The following entries give a glimpse at what goes on there. https://blogs.nasa.gov/spacestation/

December 15, 2015: New Crew Enters Station and Joins Expedition 46

Tim Kopra of NASA, Tim Peake of ESA (European Space Agency), and Yuri Malenchenko of Roscosmos joined their Expedition 46 crewmates aboard the orbiting laboratory when the hatches between the Soyuz TMA-19M spacecraft and the International Space Station officially opened at 2:58 p.m. EST. Expedition 46 Commander Scott Kelly of NASA and Flight Engineers Mikhail Kornienko and Sergey Volkov of Roscosmos welcomed the trio aboard their orbiting home.

The crew members will install equipment and conduct experiments to help NASA's journey to Mars while making discoveries that can benefit all of humanity. . . .

The incoming trio will spend about six months aboard the station. Kelly and Kornienko are about nine months into their one-year mission, and are scheduled to return home in March 2016. These trips also enable the Roscomos to rotate a crew member and a Soyuz spacecraft. Each Soyuz remains in orbit about six months.

December 16, 2015: New Crew Getting Up to Speed on the Station

The new Expedition 46 trio aboard the International Space Station is settling in for a six-month mission and getting right to work. They arrived Tuesday morning, had a quick safety briefing and rested up before their first full day aboard the orbital laboratory.

New Flight Engineers Yuri Malenchenko, Tim Kopra and Tim Peake worked throughout Wednesday familiarizing themselves with station systems and emergency procedures. During the afternoon Kopra began unloading the new Cygnus private cargo ship while Peake worked on NanoRacks gear and life support hardware. Malenchenko began unloading science experiments, including the Biosignal human cell study, and other supplies from the new Soyuz TMA-19M spacecraft. . . .

December 17, 2015: Expedition 46 Transferring Gear Before Supply Ship Undocks

The six-member Expedition 46 crew worked on human research activities and unloaded cargo today. The three newest crew members — Flight Engineers Yuri Malenchenko, Tim Kopra and Tim Peake — continued familiarizing themselves with International Space Station systems and operations.

Commander Scott Kelly used an ultrasound during the morning to scan Flight Engineer Sergey Volkov's eyes. Kelly then joined new station residents Kopra and Peake and unloaded cargo from the Cygnus private space freighter. Kelly later installed radiation detectors in the Columbus lab module. Peake filled out a daily questionnaire for the Space Headaches study.

Cosmonaut Mikhail Kornienko was in the Russian segment of the orbital lab getting the Progress 60 resupply ship ready for its undocking early Saturday morning. Malenchenko transferred gear and supplies from the new Soyuz TMA-19M spacecraft that arrived Tuesday. Malenchenko, who is on his fourth station mission, also photographed the condition of the Soyuz docking cone for inspection on the ground.

December 18, 2015: Unscheduled Spacewalk Likely on Monday

The International Space Station's mission managers are preparing for a likely unplanned spacewalk by Astronauts Scott Kelly and Tim Kopra no earlier than Monday, Dec. 21. . . .

December 19, 2015: Russian Cargo Spaceship Departs Station

A Russian resupply ship left the International Space Station today after 166 days attached to the Pirs docking compartment. The trash-filled Progress 60 (60P) undocked from Pirs at 2:35 a.m. EST/7:35 a.m. UTC and will re-enter Earth's atmosphere a few hours later for a fiery destruction over the Pacific Ocean. . . .

View from the International Space Station. Photo taken by astronaut Kimiya Yui from Japan.

The departure of the 60P this morning leaves four spacecraft docked to the orbital laboratory. The Soyuz TMA-18M crew spaceship is docked to the Poisk module. The Soyuz TMA-19M is docked to the Rassvet module. A Progress 61 cargo craft is docked to the Zvezda service module. The Cygnus private space freighter from the U.S. company Orbital ATK is berthed to the Unity module.

December 20, 2015: Station Managers "GO" For Monday Morning Spacewalk

The International Space Station Mission Management Team met Sunday and gave its approval to proceed with a spacewalk Monday out of the Quest airlock by Expedition 46 Commander Scott Kelly and Flight Engineer Tim Kopra of NASA to assist in moving the Mobile Transporter rail car a few inches to a worksite on the station's truss where it can be latched in place and electrically mated to the complex. The green light for the unplanned spacewalk to take place Monday came three days after the Mobile Transporter stalled just four inches away from its embarkation point at worksite 4 near the center of the station's truss as it began to move to another worksite to support robotic payload operations with its attached Canadarm2 robotic arm and the Special Purpose Dexterous Manipulator (Dextre). . . .

Kelly, who will be making his third spacewalk, will be extravehicular crew member 1 (EV 1) wearing the U.S. spacesuit bearing the red stripes. Kopra, who arrived on the station on Dec. 15, will be making the second spacewalk of his career as extravehicular crew member 2 (EV 2) wearing the suit with no stripes. It will be the 191st spacewalk in support of station assembly and maintenance and the seventh spacewalk of the year by station crew members.

Kelly and Kopra will float out of the Quest airlock to the area where the Mobile Transporter has stalled to check out the position of its brake handles and other mechanisms to make sure the rail car can be commanded to move back to worksite 4 by robotic flight controllers at Mission Control, Houston. It is suspected that a brake handle on an equipment cart attached to the starboard side of the transporter may have inadvertently engaged, which if correct, should easily be released to allow for the transporter to be moved into place for its latching. . . .

December 21, 2015: Astronauts Make Quick Work of Short Spacewalk

NASA astronauts Scott Kelly and Tim Kopra ended their spacewalk at 11:01 a.m. EST with the repressurization of the U.S. Quest airlock after accomplishing all objectives. They released brake handles on crew equipment carts on either side of the space station's mobile transporter rail car so it could be latched in place ahead of Wednesday's docking of a Russian cargo resupply spacecraft. The ISS Progress 62 resupply mission launched at 3:44 a.m. EST this morning (2:44 p.m. Baikonur time) from the Baikonur Cosmodrome in Kazakhstan.

After quickly completing their primary objective for the spacewalk, Kelly and Kopra tackled several get-ahead tasks. Kelly routed a second pair of cables in preparation for International Docking Adapter installment work to support U.S. commercial crew vehicles, continuing work he began during a November spacewalk. Kopra routed an Ethernet cable that ultimately will connect to a Russian laboratory module. They also retrieved tools that had been in a toolbox on the outside of the station, so they can be used for future work.

Address to the 43rd UN General Assembly Session

Mikhail Gorbachev (1988)

Gorbachev spoke to the United Nations General Assembly on December 7, 1988. He described political changes developing in the Soviet Union. He also announced that the Soviet Union was reducing its military presence in Eastern Europe. This move encouraged countries that had been under the control of the Soviet Union to work toward independence. This excerpt is from the conclusion of his speech.

We are not inclined to oversimplify the situation in the world. Yes, the tendency towards disarmament has received a strong impetus and this process is gaining its own momentum, but it has not become irreversible. Yes, the striving to give up confrontation in favour of dialogue and co-operation has made itself felt, but it has by no means secured its position forever in the practice of international relations. Yes, the movement towards a nuclear-free and non-violent world is capable of fundamentally transforming the political and spiritual face of the planet, but only the very first steps have been taken, which have moreover in certain influential circles been greeted with mistrust and are running up against resistance.

The inheritance and the inertia of the past are continuing to operate. Profound contradictions and the roots of many conflicts have not disappeared. The fundamental fact remains too that the formation of the peaceful period will take place in conditions of the existence and rivalry of various socio-economic and political systems. However, the meaning of our international efforts and one of the key tenets of the new thinking is precisely to impart to this rivalry the quality of sensible competition in conditions of respect for freedom of choice and a balance of interests.

In this case it will become even useful and productive from the viewpoint of general world development. Otherwise, if the main component remains the arms race, as it has been until now, rivalry will be fatal. Indeed an ever greater number of people throughout the world, from the man in the street to leaders, are beginning to understand this. Esteemed Mr Chairman, esteemed delegates! I finish my first speech at the UN with the same feeling with which I began it—a feeling of responsibility to my own people and to the world community. We have met at the end of a year that has been so significant for the UN and on the threshold of a year from which all of us expect so much. One would like to believe that our joint efforts to put an end to the era of wars, confrontation and regional conflicts, aggression against nature, the terror of hunger and poverty as well as political terrorism will be comparable with our hopes. This is our common goal, and it is only by acting together that we may attain it. Thank you!

Mikhail Gorbachev Addressing the UN General Assembly, 1988.

The Dayuma Story
Ethel Emily Wallis (1960)

In the early 20th century, the Waodani (or Huaorani) were an isolated people group living in the modern country of Ecuador. They had a violent culture, both among themselves and toward outsiders. Nearby tribes called them Auca, which means "savage." Dayuma (Dah-yoo'-mah) was born about 1930 into the Waorani tribe. Ethel Emily Wallis worked with Wycliffe Bible Translators. She helped promote the work of Wycliffe by writing books and articles, and she helped with Bible translation and other language projects. Wallis collaborated with Dayuma and missionary Rachel Saint on a book. Published in 1960, it was titled The Dayuma Story: Life Under Auca Spears. *The following excerpts are from the book. This first section contains Dayuma's memories about events in her tribe that prompted her to leave.*

I was born on Fish River. Afterwards we lived well on Palm River. We saw the high hills far off clearly. We saw far downriver.

My big brother was Wawae. My father was Tyaento, my mother Akawo. Nampa my brother was a small child. Oba my sister was still younger. My big sister was Onaenga, my other sister, Gimari. My mother's relatives were many. My uncles were Wamoñi and Gikita.

Moipa and Itaeka did not do well. Fleeing and hiding we came, far, far downriver. We went by canoe. Then we went back.

When did they spear? They speared at night. My father escaped into the water. They dug a grave for him and he was caused to die. But he didn't die right away. I didn't see it. They spoke and I heard. My relative said, "I buried him."

Moipa and Itaeka speared. Where did they go, did they say? On a small stream upriver we returned. We didn't see them. We drank the water of maeñika fruit. It rained. We got wet. The jaguar growled, the monkey called. We climbed the trees when the jaguar came.

Then we fled. We came at night in the moonlight. We speared gyaegyae fish. We were planting peanuts on Palm River. The outsiders came with guns and shot. Their dogs barked. We went into the water, then fled on the other side.

Dayuma later met Rachel Saint in Ecuador, and the two women became friends. This section records an exchange between Dayuma and Rachel. The Waodani did not use writing, but they did make carvings on trees to mark trails or leave signals. They referred to airplanes as "wood-bees."

Then came the day when Dayuma began to ask Rachel questions.

"Why do you want to learn my language?" With still very limited conversational ability in Auca, Rachel was on the spot. Mustering all of her available vocabulary she managed, "So that I can go to your people, and teach them not to kill, and to live well."

A wondering look was Dayuma's eloquent reply. She had understood the words—but why would anyone want to go to the killers of the forest? She herself had no intention of returning to the place from which she fled for her life.

"But if you go," she commented significantly, "see if my mother lives, see if my sister Gimari lives. Returning, you can tell me about them."

continued

Dayuma was beginning to wonder again about her family over the ridge. When she first came to the hacienda she had cried for them each night, but eventually her tears dried completely. Now Rachel's queries renewed her concern.

There were other questions brewing in the active Auca mind.

"Who sent you?" was the next challenge. Using the Auca word for God, Rachel replied, "Our God, the other God, sent me to learn from you." That was a big sentence and Rachel wondered if Dayuma understood. However, her reply was reassuring, for with a puzzled expression she said,

"It must have been your God." After a pause Dayuma then asked, "Why did you come?"

"So that I can put God's carving into your language, and teach your people what He says."

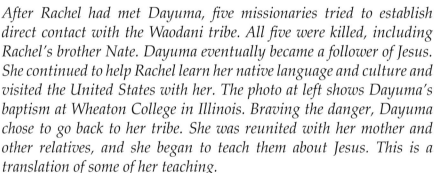

"Who taught you?"

That required a long answer. Many people in Rachel's land knew God's carving. Her mother, and her father, and her brother who flew the wood-bee knew it. Even her grandmothers and grandfathers had known, and they taught her. Now she could read God's carving for herself.

After Rachel had met Dayuma, five missionaries tried to establish direct contact with the Waodani tribe. All five were killed, including Rachel's brother Nate. Dayuma eventually became a follower of Jesus. She continued to help Rachel learn her native language and culture and visited the United States with her. The photo at left shows Dayuma's baptism at Wheaton College in Illinois. Braving the danger, Dayuma chose to go back to her tribe. She was reunited with her mother and other relatives, and she began to teach them about Jesus. This is a translation of some of her teaching.

As Easter approached Dayuma drilled her family class on the death and resurrection of Christ. The story of the raising of His dead body had never ceased to thrill her, and she emphasized it to her people, most of whom were still fearful of what would happen to dead bodies.

Gimari and Dawa listened attentively as Dayuma's animation carried her audience along with her. They hung on to every word.

"Then the followers of Jesus came and looked into the tomb—"

"*Ndae!*—There was no one!" shouted Dawa, her eyes shining with triumph. Dayuma beamed her approval, then continued with the sequel of the disciples' walk to Emmaus with the risen Christ.

"They two returned fast at night. They called out to the others, 'We have already seen Him. He is awake. We came back to tell you. He spoke to God—He is alive! We saw Him!"

"Then the others said, 'You must be talking wild. How can those who have already died be raised?'"

"Then the two said, 'Why don't you understand? It is true what they said about Him long ago. They said He would live again.' Then another said, 'One moon and one-half moon He lived there, being raised.'

"Afterward He went high up in the sky. 'Now I will go away,' He said, 'and when I go away, I will go to be beside my Father, God. Now I am going up. Afterward, in the same way, returning I will come,' He said.

"He will come again, not as a child. He will come again in the same way He went—as a Man. You say that kapok being light goes up? Like that He went up, just like kapok, rising with the wind.[*] Higher, higher, higher. Just like that. Going up, the wind takes the white fluff higher—like that, He went up. Up to the other side of the pretty clouds. Then He was not. Where did He go? They didn't see.

"Then the ones God sent, the ones who live high in the sky with God, came. 'Why do you all stay looking?' they said. 'You all in the same way will go up.' When will Jesus come? He is the One who said, 'After I go up high, I am going to come again.' Those who died long ago, believing in God, Jesus will call. Hearing, fast they will be raised. All of them, those who believed in God, will go high up in the sky.

"Now we do not know just when He will come. Day, night, sunset, midnight, dawn—we don't know. But He will come. When God says to His Son, 'Yes, now You go,' fast he will come.

"All of those who do not believe in God, all of them will be thrown out. You throw worms out of the corn. Like that God will throw them out. Do you all understand? That's how it is. Those who do not believe, the devil will take. It will be bad for all of them.

"That is how God's trail is—like that ravine over there on the other side of the river. You won't be able to cross over. Here is the devil's trail, and there is God's trail. It is a very, very beautiful trail as you go up there."

On Easter Sunday Dayuma reviewed the story. Then she challenged them directly,

"Who, and who, and who will say, 'Yes, I love God, I want to live well.' Dawa, will you?"

"Yes," said Dawa.

"Kimo?"

No reply.

"Gimari, will you?"

To her expression of consent Gimari added, "*Tomamoni!*—All of us!"

Dayuma explained that those who love God often sing to Him in remembrance of good things He has done. One refrain in an old Auca song about the God of creation would be appropriate. Thus the simple gathering ended with the Auca chant, "God created, God created everything." Then as if inspired by her own message concerning a risen Lord, Dayuma added original Auca words to the old tune:

"We say the stars shine, He created all . . .
Seeing, we will love Him in our hearts . . .
Following Jesus, to God's House we will go . . .
We will say 'No' to the devils, we all will love God."

Old and young quietly followed Dayuma's lead as each line was repeated many times.

Many Waodani eventually became Christians. Rachel Saint died in Ecuador in 1994. Dayuma died there in 2014.

---

[*] *Kapok is the name of a tropical tree and also the name for the cotton-like fluff in its seed pods.*

Turkish Protestant Church Reopens

SAT-7 (2015)

This November 20, 2015, press release is from SAT-7, an organization that broadcasts television shows by satellite in the Middle East and North Africa. Many countries with Muslim majorities limit the activity of missionaries and churches. SAT-7 produces programs for adults and children in local languages, and people can receive the programs in their homes. Februniye Akyol, age 25, was elected in 2014 as co-mayor of the city of Mardin along with Kurdish leader Ahmet Turk, age 71.

Christians of all denominations have celebrated the reopening of a Protestant church only 50 kilometres from where churches have been bombed by so-called Islamic State (IS). Located just 30 kilometres from the Syrian border, the Protestant Church in Mardin, south-eastern Turkey, rang to the praises of a packed congregation some 55 years after persecution and migration forced its closure.

Local politicians and church leaders of all denominations attended the 7 November reopening and welcomed it as a sign of the democracy and coexistence of different language and religious groups that could bring positive change to the region.

SAT-7's Turkish channel news programme filmed the event and captured a mood of faith and resolve.

Mardin Co-Mayor Februniye Akyol—herself the first Christian mayor of a Turkish city—said, "While our historic churches are being bombed and destroyed across the border, a church … coming to life in Mardin after so many years of inactivity is a message for the whole world. I hope the reopening brings hope and light to the world."

Founded in 1860 by Protestant Christians from Diyarbakir, the church originally served Assyrian Christians worshipping in Syriac or Aramaic—the language related to that spoken by Jesus.

Mardin Member of Parliament, Erol Dora, reminded worshippers that Mardin was "a city of civilisations." He said, "Our desire is that universal values of peace and wellbeing will come to our country. The opening of this church is important for universal religious freedom."

The varied worship during the church dedication was a symbol of cooperation between churches and varied ethnic backgrounds. There was exuberant Evangelical praise, unaccompanied Syriac hymns, and worship in Kurdish accompanied by baglama guitar.

SAT-7 TÜRK's news editor, Seyfi Genç, pointed out the significance. He said Orthodox churches have often refused to recognise Protestants and Kurdish people targeted Syriacs during the disputes over Cyprus in the 1970s. "Fifty years later, the Mardin Protestant church has Kurdish, Turkish and Syriac members who will worship together."

He said the Mardin church is also "one of the few legally recognised Protestant churches in Turkey," whereas most meet in homes or rented buildings and are not approved by the municipalities.

Mardin, Turkey

Behind the church's rebirth lies the vision of the Protestant Church in Diyarbakir and patient work of Pastor Ender Peker. Since being sent to Mardin by the much larger Diyarbakir fellowship two years ago, he has led meetings in a local home, built relationships with other church leaders, and overseen the restoration of a long abandoned building.

"For many years," he said, "no one knew this was a church! But now something new is beginning here. Once again, songs will be sung. Once again prayers will be heard, once again we will give God offerings and we will be united. We will serve the people of Mardin seven days a week, as the only Protestant church of the city."

Olympic Athletes

These two Olympic athletes are also Christians who want to honor God with their talents. These testimonies are reprinted with permission from Athletes in Action, the sports ministry of Cru (formerly Campus Crusade for Christ). Since they are based on interviews, some words are printed in brackets to explain something or add context.

Allyson Felix - USA

Allyson Felix started running track at high school in Los Angeles. Her older brother Wes, who also competed as a runner, now works as her agent. Felix has competed at the Olympic Games in Athens (2004), Beijing (2008), and London (2012), winning a total of four gold medals and two silver medals. Pictured at left in London, Felix is training to run again in Rio de Janeiro (2016).

My faith is definitely the most important aspect of my life. My dad is a [seminary professor] and I grew up in a very strong Christian home. Our family was very involved in our church. I am so blessed to have my family and the upbringing that I did. It means so much to me to have two very godly parents who both have so much wisdom. They are amazing role models that I have had the privilege to watch as I grew up.

I came to know Jesus Christ as my personal Savior at a very young age. Ever since then, I have continually been striving to grow in my relationship with God. I was nowhere close to the perfect child. I had my share of difficult times along with some disappointing choices that I made, but thankfully God never stops loving me.

I'm currently a work in progress and like anyone else I face struggles every day. My goal is to be more Christ-like each and every day and that is not an easy task. I know that I'm trying to be something different from [other Olympic runners] and after I run I hope that people can distinguish [Christ-like] character in the way I present myself.

I try not to focus on the pressure surrounding me. I love Philippians 4:6-7 that says, "Do not be anxious about anything, but in everything, by prayer and petition, with thanksgiving, present your requests to God. And the peace of God, which transcends all understanding, will guard your hearts and your minds in Christ Jesus." That verse always [encourages] my heart when I am dealing with any kind of pressure, and throughout the struggles of life my faith calms my heart. I try to stay in the [Bible] and I pray a lot, just talking to God. He provides my strength and wisdom.

In the season of my life that I am in now, I feel so blessed that God has given me the talent of running. My running is an amazing gift from God and I want to use it to the best of my ability to glorify Him. You have to have this passion and you have to have a reason for doing what you're doing. And there really has to be a purpose there, I think that's what drives success. I know my talent is from God. And that's my purpose: to run to glorify Him.

I'm thankful that I have been given this platform so that I can share my faith with the world!

Wilson Kipsang - Kenya

In 2013, Wilson Kipsang broke the world record for the marathon by 15 seconds. In 2014, he won both the New York and London Marathons. He won a bronze medal at the 2012 London Olympics. Pictured at right, Kipsang also hopes to compete in the 2016 Rio Olympics. This interview was conducted by Judy Nelson Lewis and Tim Pitcher.

What has assisted me most [as a runner] is where I came from. I grew up running to school and looking after cows—you have to take them a long distance. In my primary school, I really liked competing in the races. I would work hard to make sure I was in front because I'm someone who likes a challenge.

When I joined the Kenya Police Service, I began to train, and in 2007, I got my first chance to race outside of Africa. When I first started winning, I would buy a goat to slaughter and invite my neighbors to celebrate with me.

During my training time [after I joined the police service], I stayed with a friend and fellow runner named John Komen. Every Sunday he would go to church. Me, I didn't go because where I came from, there were no churches around. So he tried to motivate me, and [I started listening to him because] I could see that he's doing things the right way.

In time, I went to church [with John]. "So faith comes from hearing, and hearing by the word of Christ." (Romans 10:17 NASB). Slowly, slowly, I decided to fully dedicate my life to God. Once I did that, I began to reason in the best way and experience the favor of God. I got good results in my life because I began to approach issues the way God would want me to. I know my talent is a gift from God.

You can't go to church to win a race or ask God for prize money. God wants to see what is in your heart. God's main purpose for me is to worship and glorify His name.

Besides my friendship with John, my relationship with my pastor has really assisted me in growing [in my faith in God] and addressing issues. When I have an issue, I can always consult him. And I call him when I am traveling and we pray together.

continued

147

Now that my name is [famous], there are a lot of expectations from my community. I often ask God, "What should I control so that I can be the Kipsang you want me to be? How should I do things in the right way?"

I really want to give back to the community. A lot of athletes bring money back to assist the country to make a very big, positive improvement in every community. Now I own a hotel and I employ 25 people, and champion athletes come and train here in Iten because of the altitude and good roads.

The economic impact of a Kenyan athlete is very high. But the career of an athlete is short and uncertain, so I want to invest in the future. The children here are very sharp. They see us training; they watch us on TV working hard. We fly the flag of Kenya high. When we win, we celebrate together so they feel a part of the success.

I don't distance myself from people who don't go to church. We celebrate together. I don't want division between the community and the church. If you don't have a good relationship with your community, you cannot assist them or welcome them to church.

When I go away for a race, I ask my church to pray for me. And if I win, I buy everyone in the church a soda. This gives me an opportunity to invite my neighbors to tell them what God has done, not me.

Knowing there are lots of people cheering for me—feeling me in their hearts—becomes a really big motivator for me to keep working harder and harder. We are role models. That makes me want to break the world record [again].

The photo at left shows Kipsang training. The photo at right shows Kipsang (far right) with his pastor, Oliver Tanous (left), and his friend John Komen (center).

Index to Selections

Business and Trade

Christians and Christianity

Diaries and Journals

Education

Exploration

Europe

Games and Sports

Government and Law

Jews and Judaism

Letters

Middle East, The

Military History

Religion and Philosophy

Songs, Music, and Poetry

Technology

Image Credits

Images marked with one of these codes are used with the permission of a Creative Commons Attribution or Attribution-Share Alike License. See the websites listed for details.

CC-BY-2.0   creativecommons.org/licenses/by/2.0/
CC-BY-3.0   creativecommons.org/licenses/by/3.0/
CC-BY-SA-2.0 creativecommons.org/licenses/by-sa/2.0/
CC-BY-SA-2.5 creativecommons.org/licenses/by-sa/2.5/
CC-BY-SA-3.0 creativecommons.org/licenses/by-sa/3.0/
CC-BY-SA-3.0-AU
     creativecommons.org/licenses/by-sa/3.0/au/
CC-BY-SA-4.0 creativecommons.org/licenses/by-sa/4.0/

2	Wikimedia Commons
3	Eric Sonstroem / Flickr / CC-BY-2.0
4	Wikimedia Commons
6t	Wikimedia Commons
6b	Dmitry Denisenkov / Flickr / CC-BY-SA-2.0
7	Ed Brambley Flickr / Flickr / CC-BY-SA-2.0
8	Walters Art Museum / CC-BY-SA-3.0
9	Jebulon / Wikimedia Commons
10	Wikimedia Commons
12	Anagoria / Wikimedia Commons / CC-BY-3.0
13	J. Williams / Wikimedia Commons / CC-BY-SA-30
15	Classical Numismatic Group, Inc. (http://www.cngcoins.com) / Wikimedia Commons / CC-BY-SA-2.5
17	Los Angeles County Museum of Art (www.lacma.org)
19	Los Angeles County Museum of Art (www.lacma.org)
20	Wikimedia Commons
21	Marsyas / Wikimedia Commons CC-BY-SA-2.5
22l	Wikimedia Commons
22r	L N Roychoudhury / Wikimedia Commons / CC-BY-2.5
24	Wikimedia Commons
27	Noam Armonn / Shutterstock.com
30	Montipaiton / Shutterstock.com
31	Wikimedia Commons
32	Qfl247 / Wikimedia Commons / CC-BY-SA-30
33	Mikhail Markovskiy / Shutterstock.com
34	meunierd / Shutterstock.com
35	Wikimedia Commons
37	Olga PRaktika / Shutterstock.com
40	Rihardzz / Shutterstock.com
41	WorldWide / Shutterstock.com
43	Smithsonian Institution
47	The British Library
48	geni / Wikimedia Commons / CC-BY-SA-3.0
49	Wikimedia Commons
50	Jim McIntosh / Flickr / CC-BY-2.0
51	Wikimedia Commons
52	beggs-Brian Jeffery Beggerly / Flickr / CC-BY-2.0
54	Wikimedia Commons
56	Laborant / Shutterstock.com
58t	British Library
58b	Wikimedia Commons
59	Oleg Senkov / Shutterstock.com
60	Margoz / Wikimedia Commons / CC-BY-SA-3.0
61	Wikimedia Commons
62tl	Michal Piec / Shutterstock.com
62tr	AJP / Shutterstock.com
62bl	Byelikova Oksana / Shutterstock.com
62br	Wikimedia Commons
63tl	2630ben / Shutterstock.com
63tr	Lynn Y / Shutterstock.com
63b	2630ben / Shutterstock.com
64	Marc Ryckaert (MJJR) / Wikimedia Commons / CC-BY-3.0
65tl	Los Angeles County Museum of Art (www.lacma.org)
65tr	Los Angeles County Museum of Art (www.lacma.org)
65bl	judepics / Wikimedia Commons / CC-BY-2.0
65br	Los Angeles County Museum of Art (www.lacma.org)
66tl	Los Angeles County Museum of Art (www.lacma.org)
66tr	Wikimedia Commons
66bl	Los Angeles County Museum of Art (www.lacma.org)
66br	Numisantica (http://www.numisantica.com) / CC-BY-SA-3.0
67	Wolfgang Manousek / Flickr / CC-BY-2.0
68l	Congreso de la República del Perú / Flickr / CC-BY-2.0
68r	James Preston / Flickr / CC-BY-2.0
71	Wikimedia Commons
72	Wikimedia Commons
73	Wikimedia Commons
75	Everett Historical / Shutterstock.com
76tl	Steve Allen / Shutterstock.com
76bl	Mariusz S. Jurgielewicz / Shutterstock.com
76r	Sopotnicki / Shutterstock.com

Visit our website for more exciting homeschool curriculum
that helps you teach the heart, soul, and mind.

www.notgrass.com